FOREX TRADING JOURNAL

THIS BOOK BELONGS TO:

_____

TRADING RULES

TRADING RULES

TRADING RULES

TRADING RULES

TRADING RULES

TRADING RULES

TRADING GOALS

TRADING GOALS

TRADING GOALS

TRADING GOALS

TRADING GOALS

TRADING LOG

Order Date/Time	Pair	Order Ticket #	Buy/ Sell	Lots/ Units	Entry Price	Exit Price	Close Date/Time	Pips W/L	Profit/ Loss	New Balance

TRADE SETUP NOTES:

ADDITIONAL NOTES:

Order Date/Time	Pair	Order Ticket #	Buy/ Sell	Lots/ Units	Entry Price	Exit Price	Close Date/Time	Pips W/L	Profit/ Loss	New Balance

TRADE SETUP NOTES:

ADDITIONAL NOTES:

Order Date/Time	Pair	Order Ticket #	Buy/ Sell	Lots/ Units	Entry Price	Exit Price	Close Date/Time	Pips W/L	Profit/ Loss	New Balance

TRADE SETUP NOTES:

ADDITIONAL NOTES:

Order Date/Time	Pair	Order Ticket #	Buy/ Sell	Lots/ Units	Entry Price	Exit Price	Close Date/Time	Pips W/L	Profit/ Loss	New Balance

TRADE SETUP NOTES:

ADDITIONAL NOTES:

Order Date/Time	Pair	Order Ticket #	Buy/ Sell	Lots/ Units	Entry Price	Exit Price	Close Date/Time	Pips W/L	Profit/ Loss	New Balance

TRADE SETUP NOTES:

ADDITIONAL NOTES:

Order Date/Time	Pair	Order Ticket #	Buy/ Sell	Lots/ Units	Entry Price	Exit Price	Close Date/Time	Pips W/L	Profit/ Loss	New Balance

TRADE SETUP NOTES:

ADDITIONAL NOTES:

Order Date/Time	Pair	Order Ticket #	Buy/ Sell	Lots/ Units	Entry Price	Exit Price	Close Date/Time	Pips W/L	Profit/ Loss	New Balance

TRADE SETUP NOTES:

ADDITIONAL NOTES:

TRADING LOG

Order Date/Time	Pair	Order Ticket #	Buy/ Sell	Lots/ Units	Entry Price	Exit Price	Close Date/Time	Pips W/L	Profit/ Loss	New Balance

TRADE SETUP NOTES:

ADDITIONAl NOTES:

Order Date/Time	Pair	Order Ticket #	Buy/ Sell	Lots/ Units	Entry Price	Exit Price	Close Date/Time	Pips W/L	Profit/ Loss	New Balance

TRADE SETUP NOTES:

ADDITIONAl NOTES:

Order Date/Time	Pair	Order Ticket #	Buy/ Sell	Lots/ Units	Entry Price	Exit Price	Close Date/Time	Pips W/L	Profit/ Loss	New Balance

TRADE SETUP NOTES:

ADDITIONAl NOTES:

Order Date/Time	Pair	Order Ticket #	Buy/ Sell	Lots/ Units	Entry Price	Exit Price	Close Date/Time	Pips W/L	Profit/ Loss	New Balance

TRADE SETUP NOTES:

ADDITIONAl NOTES:

Order Date/Time	Pair	Order Ticket #	Buy/ Sell	Lots/ Units	Entry Price	Exit Price	Close Date/Time	Pips W/L	Profit/ Loss	New Balance

TRADE SETUP NOTES:

ADDITIONAl NOTES:

Order Date/Time	Pair	Order Ticket #	Buy/ Sell	Lots/ Units	Entry Price	Exit Price	Close Date/Time	Pips W/L	Profit/ Loss	New Balance

TRADE SETUP NOTES:

ADDITIONAl NOTES:

TRADING LOG

Order Date/Time	Pair	Order Ticket #	Buy/ Sell	Lots/ Units	Entry Price	Exit Price	Close Date/Time	Pips W/L	Profit/ Loss	New Balance

TRADE SETUP NOTES:

ADDITIONAL NOTES:

Order Date/Time	Pair	Order Ticket #	Buy/ Sell	Lots/ Units	Entry Price	Exit Price	Close Date/Time	Pips W/L	Profit/ Loss	New Balance

TRADE SETUP NOTES:

ADDITIONAL NOTES:

Order Date/Time	Pair	Order Ticket #	Buy/ Sell	Lots/ Units	Entry Price	Exit Price	Close Date/Time	Pips W/L	Profit/ Loss	New Balance

TRADE SETUP NOTES:

ADDITIONAL NOTES:

Order Date/Time	Pair	Order Ticket #	Buy/ Sell	Lots/ Units	Entry Price	Exit Price	Close Date/Time	Pips W/L	Profit/ Loss	New Balance

TRADE SETUP NOTES:

ADDITIONAL NOTES:

Order Date/Time	Pair	Order Ticket #	Buy/ Sell	Lots/ Units	Entry Price	Exit Price	Close Date/Time	Pips W/L	Profit/ Loss	New Balance

TRADE SETUP NOTES:

ADDITIONAL NOTES:

Order Date/Time	Pair	Order Ticket #	Buy/ Sell	Lots/ Units	Entry Price	Exit Price	Close Date/Time	Pips W/L	Profit/ Loss	New Balance

TRADE SETUP NOTES:

ADDITIONAL NOTES:

Order Date/Time	Pair	Order Ticket #	Buy/ Sell	Lots/ Units	Entry Price	Exit Price	Close Date/Time	Pips W/L	Profit/ Loss	New Balance

TRADE SETUP NOTES:

ADDITIONAL NOTES:

TRADING LOG

Order Date/Time	Pair	Order Ticket #	Buy/ Sell	Lots/ Units	Entry Price	Exit Price	Close Date/Time	Pips W/L	Profit/ Loss	New Balance

TRADE SETUP NOTES:

ADDITIONAl NOTES:

Order Date/Time	Pair	Order Ticket #	Buy/ Sell	Lots/ Units	Entry Price	Exit Price	Close Date/Time	Pips W/L	Profit/ Loss	New Balance

TRADE SETUP NOTES:

ADDITIONAl NOTES:

Order Date/Time	Pair	Order Ticket #	Buy/ Sell	Lots/ Units	Entry Price	Exit Price	Close Date/Time	Pips W/L	Profit/ Loss	New Balance

TRADE SETUP NOTES:

ADDITIONAl NOTES:

Order Date/Time	Pair	Order Ticket #	Buy/ Sell	Lots/ Units	Entry Price	Exit Price	Close Date/Time	Pips W/L	Profit/ Loss	New Balance

TRADE SETUP NOTES:

ADDITIONAl NOTES:

Order Date/Time	Pair	Order Ticket #	Buy/ Sell	Lots/ Units	Entry Price	Exit Price	Close Date/Time	Pips W/L	Profit/ Loss	New Balance

TRADE SETUP NOTES:

ADDITIONAl NOTES:

Order Date/Time	Pair	Order Ticket #	Buy/ Sell	Lots/ Units	Entry Price	Exit Price	Close Date/Time	Pips W/L	Profit/ Loss	New Balance

TRADE SETUP NOTES:

ADDITIONAl NOTES:

TRADING LOG

Order Date/Time	Pair	Order Ticket #	Buy/ Sell	Lots/ Units	Entry Price	Exit Price	Close Date/Time	Pips W/L	Profit/ Loss	New Balance

TRADE SETUP NOTES:

ADDITIONAL NOTES:

Order Date/Time	Pair	Order Ticket #	Buy/ Sell	Lots/ Units	Entry Price	Exit Price	Close Date/Time	Pips W/L	Profit/ Loss	New Balance

TRADE SETUP NOTES:

ADDITIONAL NOTES:

Order Date/Time	Pair	Order Ticket #	Buy/ Sell	Lots/ Units	Entry Price	Exit Price	Close Date/Time	Pips W/L	Profit/ Loss	New Balance

TRADE SETUP NOTES:

ADDITIONAL NOTES:

Order Date/Time	Pair	Order Ticket #	Buy/ Sell	Lots/ Units	Entry Price	Exit Price	Close Date/Time	Pips W/L	Profit/ Loss	New Balance

TRADE SETUP NOTES:

ADDITIONAL NOTES:

Order Date/Time	Pair	Order Ticket #	Buy/ Sell	Lots/ Units	Entry Price	Exit Price	Close Date/Time	Pips W/L	Profit/ Loss	New Balance

TRADE SETUP NOTES:

ADDITIONAL NOTES:

Order Date/Time	Pair	Order Ticket #	Buy/ Sell	Lots/ Units	Entry Price	Exit Price	Close Date/Time	Pips W/L	Profit/ Loss	New Balance

TRADE SETUP NOTES:

ADDITIONAL NOTES:

Order Date/Time	Pair	Order Ticket #	Buy/ Sell	Lots/ Units	Entry Price	Exit Price	Close Date/Time	Pips W/L	Profit/ Loss	New Balance

TRADE SETUP NOTES:

ADDITIONAL NOTES:

TRADING LOG

Order Date/Time	Pair	Order Ticket #	Buy/ Sell	Lots/ Units	Entry Price	Exit Price	Close Date/Time	Pips W/L	Profit/ Loss	New Balance

TRADE SETUP NOTES:

ADDITIONAL NOTES:

Order Date/Time	Pair	Order Ticket #	Buy/ Sell	Lots/ Units	Entry Price	Exit Price	Close Date/Time	Pips W/L	Profit/ Loss	New Balance

TRADE SETUP NOTES:

ADDITIONAL NOTES:

Order Date/Time	Pair	Order Ticket #	Buy/ Sell	Lots/ Units	Entry Price	Exit Price	Close Date/Time	Pips W/L	Profit/ Loss	New Balance

TRADE SETUP NOTES:

ADDITIONAL NOTES:

Order Date/Time	Pair	Order Ticket #	Buy/ Sell	Lots/ Units	Entry Price	Exit Price	Close Date/Time	Pips W/L	Profit/ Loss	New Balance

TRADE SETUP NOTES:

ADDITIONAL NOTES:

Order Date/Time	Pair	Order Ticket #	Buy/ Sell	Lots/ Units	Entry Price	Exit Price	Close Date/Time	Pips W/L	Profit/ Loss	New Balance

TRADE SETUP NOTES:

ADDITIONAL NOTES:

Order Date/Time	Pair	Order Ticket #	Buy/ Sell	Lots/ Units	Entry Price	Exit Price	Close Date/Time	Pips W/L	Profit/ Loss	New Balance

TRADE SETUP NOTES:

ADDITIONAL NOTES:

TRADING LOG

Order Date/Time	Pair	Order Ticket #	Buy/ Sell	Lots/ Units	Entry Price	Exit Price	Close Date/Time	Pips W/L	Profit/ Loss	New Balance

TRADE SETUP NOTES:

ADDITIONAl NOTES:

Order Date/Time	Pair	Order Ticket #	Buy/ Sell	Lots/ Units	Entry Price	Exit Price	Close Date/Time	Pips W/L	Profit/ Loss	New Balance

TRADE SETUP NOTES:

ADDITIONAl NOTES:

Order Date/Time	Pair	Order Ticket #	Buy/ Sell	Lots/ Units	Entry Price	Exit Price	Close Date/Time	Pips W/L	Profit/ Loss	New Balance

TRADE SETUP NOTES:

ADDITIONAl NOTES:

Order Date/Time	Pair	Order Ticket #	Buy/ Sell	Lots/ Units	Entry Price	Exit Price	Close Date/Time	Pips W/L	Profit/ Loss	New Balance

TRADE SETUP NOTES:

ADDITIONAl NOTES:

Order Date/Time	Pair	Order Ticket #	Buy/ Sell	Lots/ Units	Entry Price	Exit Price	Close Date/Time	Pips W/L	Profit/ Loss	New Balance

TRADE SETUP NOTES:

ADDITIONAl NOTES:

Order Date/Time	Pair	Order Ticket #	Buy/ Sell	Lots/ Units	Entry Price	Exit Price	Close Date/Time	Pips W/L	Profit/ Loss	New Balance

TRADE SETUP NOTES:

ADDITIONAl NOTES:

Order Date/Time	Pair	Order Ticket #	Buy/ Sell	Lots/ Units	Entry Price	Exit Price	Close Date/Time	Pips W/L	Profit/ Loss	New Balance

TRADE SETUP NOTES:

ADDITIONAl NOTES:

TRADING LOG

Order Date/Time	Pair	Order Ticket #	Buy/ Sell	Lots/ Units	Entry Price	Exit Price	Close Date/Time	Pips W/L	Profit/ Loss	New Balance

TRADE SETUP NOTES:

ADDITIONAL NOTES:

Order Date/Time	Pair	Order Ticket #	Buy/ Sell	Lots/ Units	Entry Price	Exit Price	Close Date/Time	Pips W/L	Profit/ Loss	New Balance

TRADE SETUP NOTES:

ADDITIONAL NOTES:

Order Date/Time	Pair	Order Ticket #	Buy/ Sell	Lots/ Units	Entry Price	Exit Price	Close Date/Time	Pips W/L	Profit/ Loss	New Balance

TRADE SETUP NOTES:

ADDITIONAL NOTES:

Order Date/Time	Pair	Order Ticket #	Buy/ Sell	Lots/ Units	Entry Price	Exit Price	Close Date/Time	Pips W/L	Profit/ Loss	New Balance

TRADE SETUP NOTES:

ADDITIONAL NOTES:

Order Date/Time	Pair	Order Ticket #	Buy/ Sell	Lots/ Units	Entry Price	Exit Price	Close Date/Time	Pips W/L	Profit/ Loss	New Balance

TRADE SETUP NOTES:

ADDITIONAL NOTES:

Order Date/Time	Pair	Order Ticket #	Buy/ Sell	Lots/ Units	Entry Price	Exit Price	Close Date/Time	Pips W/L	Profit/ Loss	New Balance

TRADE SETUP NOTES:

ADDITIONAL NOTES:

TRADING LOG

Order Date/Time	Pair	Order Ticket #	Buy/ Sell	Lots/ Units	Entry Price	Exit Price	Close Date/Time	Pips W/L	Profit/ Loss	New Balance

TRADE SETUP NOTES:

ADDITIONAl NOTES:

Order Date/Time	Pair	Order Ticket #	Buy/ Sell	Lots/ Units	Entry Price	Exit Price	Close Date/Time	Pips W/L	Profit/ Loss	New Balance

TRADE SETUP NOTES:

ADDITIONAl NOTES:

Order Date/Time	Pair	Order Ticket #	Buy/ Sell	Lots/ Units	Entry Price	Exit Price	Close Date/Time	Pips W/L	Profit/ Loss	New Balance

TRADE SETUP NOTES:

ADDITIONAl NOTES:

Order Date/Time	Pair	Order Ticket #	Buy/ Sell	Lots/ Units	Entry Price	Exit Price	Close Date/Time	Pips W/L	Profit/ Loss	New Balance

TRADE SETUP NOTES:

ADDITIONAl NOTES:

Order Date/Time	Pair	Order Ticket #	Buy/ Sell	Lots/ Units	Entry Price	Exit Price	Close Date/Time	Pips W/L	Profit/ Loss	New Balance

TRADE SETUP NOTES:

ADDITIONAl NOTES:

Order Date/Time	Pair	Order Ticket #	Buy/ Sell	Lots/ Units	Entry Price	Exit Price	Close Date/Time	Pips W/L	Profit/ Loss	New Balance

TRADE SETUP NOTES:

ADDITIONAl NOTES:

Order Date/Time	Pair	Order Ticket #	Buy/ Sell	Lots/ Units	Entry Price	Exit Price	Close Date/Time	Pips W/L	Profit/ Loss	New Balance

TRADE SETUP NOTES:

ADDITIONAl NOTES:

TRADING LOG

Order Date/Time	Pair	Order Ticket #	Buy/ Sell	Lots/ Units	Entry Price	Exit Price	Close Date/Time	Pips W/L	Profit/ Loss	New Balance

TRADE SETUP NOTES:

ADDITIONAl NOTES:

Order Date/Time	Pair	Order Ticket #	Buy/ Sell	Lots/ Units	Entry Price	Exit Price	Close Date/Time	Pips W/L	Profit/ Loss	New Balance

TRADE SETUP NOTES:

ADDITIONAl NOTES:

Order Date/Time	Pair	Order Ticket #	Buy/ Sell	Lots/ Units	Entry Price	Exit Price	Close Date/Time	Pips W/L	Profit/ Loss	New Balance

TRADE SETUP NOTES:

ADDITIONAl NOTES:

Order Date/Time	Pair	Order Ticket #	Buy/ Sell	Lots/ Units	Entry Price	Exit Price	Close Date/Time	Pips W/L	Profit/ Loss	New Balance

TRADE SETUP NOTES:

ADDITIONAl NOTES:

Order Date/Time	Pair	Order Ticket #	Buy/ Sell	Lots/ Units	Entry Price	Exit Price	Close Date/Time	Pips W/L	Profit/ Loss	New Balance

TRADE SETUP NOTES:

ADDITIONAl NOTES:

Order Date/Time	Pair	Order Ticket #	Buy/ Sell	Lots/ Units	Entry Price	Exit Price	Close Date/Time	Pips W/L	Profit/ Loss	New Balance

TRADE SETUP NOTES:

ADDITIONAl NOTES:

TRADING LOG

Order Date/Time	Pair	Order Ticket #	Buy/ Sell	Lots/ Units	Entry Price	Exit Price	Close Date/Time	Pips W/L	Profit/ Loss	New Balance

TRADE SETUP NOTES:

ADDITIONAL NOTES:

Order Date/Time	Pair	Order Ticket #	Buy/ Sell	Lots/ Units	Entry Price	Exit Price	Close Date/Time	Pips W/L	Profit/ Loss	New Balance

TRADE SETUP NOTES:

ADDITIONAL NOTES:

Order Date/Time	Pair	Order Ticket #	Buy/ Sell	Lots/ Units	Entry Price	Exit Price	Close Date/Time	Pips W/L	Profit/ Loss	New Balance

TRADE SETUP NOTES:

ADDITIONAL NOTES:

Order Date/Time	Pair	Order Ticket #	Buy/ Sell	Lots/ Units	Entry Price	Exit Price	Close Date/Time	Pips W/L	Profit/ Loss	New Balance

TRADE SETUP NOTES:

ADDITIONAL NOTES:

Order Date/Time	Pair	Order Ticket #	Buy/ Sell	Lots/ Units	Entry Price	Exit Price	Close Date/Time	Pips W/L	Profit/ Loss	New Balance

TRADE SETUP NOTES:

ADDITIONAL NOTES:

Order Date/Time	Pair	Order Ticket #	Buy/ Sell	Lots/ Units	Entry Price	Exit Price	Close Date/Time	Pips W/L	Profit/ Loss	New Balance

TRADE SETUP NOTES:

ADDITIONAL NOTES:

Order Date/Time	Pair	Order Ticket #	Buy/ Sell	Lots/ Units	Entry Price	Exit Price	Close Date/Time	Pips W/L	Profit/ Loss	New Balance

TRADE SETUP NOTES:

ADDITIONAL NOTES:

TRADING LOG

Order Date/Time	Pair	Order Ticket #	Buy/ Sell	Lots/ Units	Entry Price	Exit Price	Close Date/Time	Pips W/L	Profit/ Loss	New Balance

TRADE SETUP NOTES:

ADDITIONAl NOTES:

Order Date/Time	Pair	Order Ticket #	Buy/ Sell	Lots/ Units	Entry Price	Exit Price	Close Date/Time	Pips W/L	Profit/ Loss	New Balance

TRADE SETUP NOTES:

ADDITIONAl NOTES:

Order Date/Time	Pair	Order Ticket #	Buy/ Sell	Lots/ Units	Entry Price	Exit Price	Close Date/Time	Pips W/L	Profit/ Loss	New Balance

TRADE SETUP NOTES:

ADDITIONAl NOTES:

Order Date/Time	Pair	Order Ticket #	Buy/ Sell	Lots/ Units	Entry Price	Exit Price	Close Date/Time	Pips W/L	Profit/ Loss	New Balance

TRADE SETUP NOTES:

ADDITIONAl NOTES:

Order Date/Time	Pair	Order Ticket #	Buy/ Sell	Lots/ Units	Entry Price	Exit Price	Close Date/Time	Pips W/L	Profit/ Loss	New Balance

TRADE SETUP NOTES:

ADDITIONAl NOTES:

Order Date/Time	Pair	Order Ticket #	Buy/ Sell	Lots/ Units	Entry Price	Exit Price	Close Date/Time	Pips W/L	Profit/ Loss	New Balance

TRADE SETUP NOTES:

ADDITIONAl NOTES:

Order Date/Time	Pair	Order Ticket #	Buy/ Sell	Lots/ Units	Entry Price	Exit Price	Close Date/Time	Pips W/L	Profit/ Loss	New Balance

TRADE SETUP NOTES:

ADDITIONAl NOTES:

TRADING LOG

Order Date/Time	Pair	Order Ticket #	Buy/ Sell	Lots/ Units	Entry Price	Exit Price	Close Date/Time	Pips W/L	Profit/ Loss	New Balance

TRADE SETUP NOTES:

ADDITIONAL NOTES:

Order Date/Time	Pair	Order Ticket #	Buy/ Sell	Lots/ Units	Entry Price	Exit Price	Close Date/Time	Pips W/L	Profit/ Loss	New Balance

TRADE SETUP NOTES:

ADDITIONAL NOTES:

Order Date/Time	Pair	Order Ticket #	Buy/ Sell	Lots/ Units	Entry Price	Exit Price	Close Date/Time	Pips W/L	Profit/ Loss	New Balance

TRADE SETUP NOTES:

ADDITIONAL NOTES:

Order Date/Time	Pair	Order Ticket #	Buy/ Sell	Lots/ Units	Entry Price	Exit Price	Close Date/Time	Pips W/L	Profit/ Loss	New Balance

TRADE SETUP NOTES:

ADDITIONAL NOTES:

Order Date/Time	Pair	Order Ticket #	Buy/ Sell	Lots/ Units	Entry Price	Exit Price	Close Date/Time	Pips W/L	Profit/ Loss	New Balance

TRADE SETUP NOTES:

ADDITIONAL NOTES:

Order Date/Time	Pair	Order Ticket #	Buy/ Sell	Lots/ Units	Entry Price	Exit Price	Close Date/Time	Pips W/L	Profit/ Loss	New Balance

TRADE SETUP NOTES:

ADDITIONAL NOTES:

Order Date/Time	Pair	Order Ticket #	Buy/ Sell	Lots/ Units	Entry Price	Exit Price	Close Date/Time	Pips W/L	Profit/ Loss	New Balance

TRADE SETUP NOTES:

ADDITIONAL NOTES:

TRADING LOG

Order Date/Time	Pair	Order Ticket #	Buy/ Sell	Lots/ Units	Entry Price	Exit Price	Close Date/Time	Pips W/L	Profit/ Loss	New Balance

TRADE SETUP NOTES:

ADDITIONAL NOTES:

Order Date/Time	Pair	Order Ticket #	Buy/ Sell	Lots/ Units	Entry Price	Exit Price	Close Date/Time	Pips W/L	Profit/ Loss	New Balance

TRADE SETUP NOTES:

ADDITIONAL NOTES:

Order Date/Time	Pair	Order Ticket #	Buy/ Sell	Lots/ Units	Entry Price	Exit Price	Close Date/Time	Pips W/L	Profit/ Loss	New Balance

TRADE SETUP NOTES:

ADDITIONAL NOTES:

Order Date/Time	Pair	Order Ticket #	Buy/ Sell	Lots/ Units	Entry Price	Exit Price	Close Date/Time	Pips W/L	Profit/ Loss	New Balance

TRADE SETUP NOTES:

ADDITIONAL NOTES:

Order Date/Time	Pair	Order Ticket #	Buy/ Sell	Lots/ Units	Entry Price	Exit Price	Close Date/Time	Pips W/L	Profit/ Loss	New Balance

TRADE SETUP NOTES:

ADDITIONAL NOTES:

Order Date/Time	Pair	Order Ticket #	Buy/ Sell	Lots/ Units	Entry Price	Exit Price	Close Date/Time	Pips W/L	Profit/ Loss	New Balance

TRADE SETUP NOTES:

ADDITIONAL NOTES:

TRADING LOG

Order Date/Time	Pair	Order Ticket #	Buy/ Sell	Lots/ Units	Entry Price	Exit Price	Close Date/Time	Pips W/L	Profit/ Loss	New Balance

TRADE SETUP NOTES:

ADDITIONAl NOTES:

Order Date/Time	Pair	Order Ticket #	Buy/ Sell	Lots/ Units	Entry Price	Exit Price	Close Date/Time	Pips W/L	Profit/ Loss	New Balance

TRADE SETUP NOTES:

ADDITIONAl NOTES:

Order Date/Time	Pair	Order Ticket #	Buy/ Sell	Lots/ Units	Entry Price	Exit Price	Close Date/Time	Pips W/L	Profit/ Loss	New Balance

TRADE SETUP NOTES:

ADDITIONAl NOTES:

Order Date/Time	Pair	Order Ticket #	Buy/ Sell	Lots/ Units	Entry Price	Exit Price	Close Date/Time	Pips W/L	Profit/ Loss	New Balance

TRADE SETUP NOTES:

ADDITIONAl NOTES:

Order Date/Time	Pair	Order Ticket #	Buy/ Sell	Lots/ Units	Entry Price	Exit Price	Close Date/Time	Pips W/L	Profit/ Loss	New Balance

TRADE SETUP NOTES:

ADDITIONAl NOTES:

Order Date/Time	Pair	Order Ticket #	Buy/ Sell	Lots/ Units	Entry Price	Exit Price	Close Date/Time	Pips W/L	Profit/ Loss	New Balance

TRADE SETUP NOTES:

ADDITIONAl NOTES:

Order Date/Time	Pair	Order Ticket #	Buy/ Sell	Lots/ Units	Entry Price	Exit Price	Close Date/Time	Pips W/L	Profit/ Loss	New Balance

TRADE SETUP NOTES:

ADDITIONAl NOTES:

TRADING LOG

Order Date/Time	Pair	Order Ticket #	Buy/ Sell	Lots/ Units	Entry Price	Exit Price	Close Date/Time	Pips W/L	Profit/ Loss	New Balance

TRADE SETUP NOTES:

ADDITIONAl NOTES:

Order Date/Time	Pair	Order Ticket #	Buy/ Sell	Lots/ Units	Entry Price	Exit Price	Close Date/Time	Pips W/L	Profit/ Loss	New Balance

TRADE SETUP NOTES:

ADDITIONAl NOTES:

Order Date/Time	Pair	Order Ticket #	Buy/ Sell	Lots/ Units	Entry Price	Exit Price	Close Date/Time	Pips W/L	Profit/ Loss	New Balance

TRADE SETUP NOTES:

ADDITIONAl NOTES:

Order Date/Time	Pair	Order Ticket #	Buy/ Sell	Lots/ Units	Entry Price	Exit Price	Close Date/Time	Pips W/L	Profit/ Loss	New Balance

TRADE SETUP NOTES:

ADDITIONAl NOTES:

Order Date/Time	Pair	Order Ticket #	Buy/ Sell	Lots/ Units	Entry Price	Exit Price	Close Date/Time	Pips W/L	Profit/ Loss	New Balance

TRADE SETUP NOTES:

ADDITIONAl NOTES:

Order Date/Time	Pair	Order Ticket #	Buy/ Sell	Lots/ Units	Entry Price	Exit Price	Close Date/Time	Pips W/L	Profit/ Loss	New Balance

TRADE SETUP NOTES:

ADDITIONAl NOTES:

TRADING LOG

Order Date/Time	Pair	Order Ticket #	Buy/ Sell	Lots/ Units	Entry Price	Exit Price	Close Date/Time	Pips W/L	Profit/ Loss	New Balance

TRADE SETUP NOTES:
ADDITIONAL NOTES:

Order Date/Time	Pair	Order Ticket #	Buy/ Sell	Lots/ Units	Entry Price	Exit Price	Close Date/Time	Pips W/L	Profit/ Loss	New Balance

TRADE SETUP NOTES:
ADDITIONAL NOTES:

Order Date/Time	Pair	Order Ticket #	Buy/ Sell	Lots/ Units	Entry Price	Exit Price	Close Date/Time	Pips W/L	Profit/ Loss	New Balance

TRADE SETUP NOTES:
ADDITIONAL NOTES:

Order Date/Time	Pair	Order Ticket #	Buy/ Sell	Lots/ Units	Entry Price	Exit Price	Close Date/Time	Pips W/L	Profit/ Loss	New Balance

TRADE SETUP NOTES:
ADDITIONAL NOTES:

Order Date/Time	Pair	Order Ticket #	Buy/ Sell	Lots/ Units	Entry Price	Exit Price	Close Date/Time	Pips W/L	Profit/ Loss	New Balance

TRADE SETUP NOTES:
ADDITIONAL NOTES:

Order Date/Time	Pair	Order Ticket #	Buy/ Sell	Lots/ Units	Entry Price	Exit Price	Close Date/Time	Pips W/L	Profit/ Loss	New Balance

TRADE SETUP NOTES:
ADDITIONAL NOTES:

Order Date/Time	Pair	Order Ticket #	Buy/ Sell	Lots/ Units	Entry Price	Exit Price	Close Date/Time	Pips W/L	Profit/ Loss	New Balance

TRADE SETUP NOTES:
ADDITIONAL NOTES:

TRADING LOG

Order Date/Time	Pair	Order Ticket #	Buy/ Sell	Lots/ Units	Entry Price	Exit Price	Close Date/Time	Pips W/L	Profit/ Loss	New Balance

TRADE SETUP NOTES:

ADDITIONAl NOTES:

Order Date/Time	Pair	Order Ticket #	Buy/ Sell	Lots/ Units	Entry Price	Exit Price	Close Date/Time	Pips W/L	Profit/ Loss	New Balance

TRADE SETUP NOTES:

ADDITIONAl NOTES:

Order Date/Time	Pair	Order Ticket #	Buy/ Sell	Lots/ Units	Entry Price	Exit Price	Close Date/Time	Pips W/L	Profit/ Loss	New Balance

TRADE SETUP NOTES:

ADDITIONAl NOTES:

Order Date/Time	Pair	Order Ticket #	Buy/ Sell	Lots/ Units	Entry Price	Exit Price	Close Date/Time	Pips W/L	Profit/ Loss	New Balance

TRADE SETUP NOTES:

ADDITIONAl NOTES:

Order Date/Time	Pair	Order Ticket #	Buy/ Sell	Lots/ Units	Entry Price	Exit Price	Close Date/Time	Pips W/L	Profit/ Loss	New Balance

TRADE SETUP NOTES:

ADDITIONAl NOTES:

Order Date/Time	Pair	Order Ticket #	Buy/ Sell	Lots/ Units	Entry Price	Exit Price	Close Date/Time	Pips W/L	Profit/ Loss	New Balance

TRADE SETUP NOTES:

ADDITIONAl NOTES:

TRADING LOG

Order Date/Time	Pair	Order Ticket #	Buy/ Sell	Lots/ Units	Entry Price	Exit Price	Close Date/Time	Pips W/L	Profit/ Loss	New Balance

TRADE SETUP NOTES:

ADDITIONAl NOTES:

Order Date/Time	Pair	Order Ticket #	Buy/ Sell	Lots/ Units	Entry Price	Exit Price	Close Date/Time	Pips W/L	Profit/ Loss	New Balance

TRADE SETUP NOTES:

ADDITIONAl NOTES:

Order Date/Time	Pair	Order Ticket #	Buy/ Sell	Lots/ Units	Entry Price	Exit Price	Close Date/Time	Pips W/L	Profit/ Loss	New Balance

TRADE SETUP NOTES:

ADDITIONAl NOTES:

Order Date/Time	Pair	Order Ticket #	Buy/ Sell	Lots/ Units	Entry Price	Exit Price	Close Date/Time	Pips W/L	Profit/ Loss	New Balance

TRADE SETUP NOTES:

ADDITIONAl NOTES:

Order Date/Time	Pair	Order Ticket #	Buy/ Sell	Lots/ Units	Entry Price	Exit Price	Close Date/Time	Pips W/L	Profit/ Loss	New Balance

TRADE SETUP NOTES:

ADDITIONAl NOTES:

Order Date/Time	Pair	Order Ticket #	Buy/ Sell	Lots/ Units	Entry Price	Exit Price	Close Date/Time	Pips W/L	Profit/ Loss	New Balance

TRADE SETUP NOTES:

ADDITIONAl NOTES:

Order Date/Time	Pair	Order Ticket #	Buy/ Sell	Lots/ Units	Entry Price	Exit Price	Close Date/Time	Pips W/L	Profit/ Loss	New Balance

TRADE SETUP NOTES:

ADDITIONAl NOTES:

TRADING LOG

Order Date/Time	Pair	Order Ticket #	Buy/ Sell	Lots/ Units	Entry Price	Exit Price	Close Date/Time	Pips W/L	Profit/ Loss	New Balance

TRADE SETUP NOTES:

ADDITIONAL NOTES:

Order Date/Time	Pair	Order Ticket #	Buy/ Sell	Lots/ Units	Entry Price	Exit Price	Close Date/Time	Pips W/L	Profit/ Loss	New Balance

TRADE SETUP NOTES:

ADDITIONAL NOTES:

Order Date/Time	Pair	Order Ticket #	Buy/ Sell	Lots/ Units	Entry Price	Exit Price	Close Date/Time	Pips W/L	Profit/ Loss	New Balance

TRADE SETUP NOTES:

ADDITIONAL NOTES:

Order Date/Time	Pair	Order Ticket #	Buy/ Sell	Lots/ Units	Entry Price	Exit Price	Close Date/Time	Pips W/L	Profit/ Loss	New Balance

TRADE SETUP NOTES:

ADDITIONAL NOTES:

Order Date/Time	Pair	Order Ticket #	Buy/ Sell	Lots/ Units	Entry Price	Exit Price	Close Date/Time	Pips W/L	Profit/ Loss	New Balance

TRADE SETUP NOTES:

ADDITIONAL NOTES:

Order Date/Time	Pair	Order Ticket #	Buy/ Sell	Lots/ Units	Entry Price	Exit Price	Close Date/Time	Pips W/L	Profit/ Loss	New Balance

TRADE SETUP NOTES:

ADDITIONAL NOTES:

Order Date/Time	Pair	Order Ticket #	Buy/ Sell	Lots/ Units	Entry Price	Exit Price	Close Date/Time	Pips W/L	Profit/ Loss	New Balance

TRADE SETUP NOTES:

ADDITIONAL NOTES:

TRADING LOG

Order Date/Time	Pair	Order Ticket #	Buy/ Sell	Lots/ Units	Entry Price	Exit Price	Close Date/Time	Pips W/L	Profit/ Loss	New Balance

TRADE SETUP NOTES:

ADDITIONAl NOTES:

Order Date/Time	Pair	Order Ticket #	Buy/ Sell	Lots/ Units	Entry Price	Exit Price	Close Date/Time	Pips W/L	Profit/ Loss	New Balance

TRADE SETUP NOTES:

ADDITIONAl NOTES:

Order Date/Time	Pair	Order Ticket #	Buy/ Sell	Lots/ Units	Entry Price	Exit Price	Close Date/Time	Pips W/L	Profit/ Loss	New Balance

TRADE SETUP NOTES:

ADDITIONAl NOTES:

Order Date/Time	Pair	Order Ticket #	Buy/ Sell	Lots/ Units	Entry Price	Exit Price	Close Date/Time	Pips W/L	Profit/ Loss	New Balance

TRADE SETUP NOTES:

ADDITIONAl NOTES:

Order Date/Time	Pair	Order Ticket #	Buy/ Sell	Lots/ Units	Entry Price	Exit Price	Close Date/Time	Pips W/L	Profit/ Loss	New Balance

TRADE SETUP NOTES:

ADDITIONAl NOTES:

Order Date/Time	Pair	Order Ticket #	Buy/ Sell	Lots/ Units	Entry Price	Exit Price	Close Date/Time	Pips W/L	Profit/ Loss	New Balance

TRADE SETUP NOTES:

ADDITIONAl NOTES:

Order Date/Time	Pair	Order Ticket #	Buy/ Sell	Lots/ Units	Entry Price	Exit Price	Close Date/Time	Pips W/L	Profit/ Loss	New Balance

TRADE SETUP NOTES:

ADDITIONAl NOTES:

TRADING LOG

Order Date/Time	Pair	Order Ticket #	Buy/ Sell	Lots/ Units	Entry Price	Exit Price	Close Date/Time	Pips W/L	Profit/ Loss	New Balance

TRADE SETUP NOTES:

ADDITIONAL NOTES:

Order Date/Time	Pair	Order Ticket #	Buy/ Sell	Lots/ Units	Entry Price	Exit Price	Close Date/Time	Pips W/L	Profit/ Loss	New Balance

TRADE SETUP NOTES:

ADDITIONAL NOTES:

Order Date/Time	Pair	Order Ticket #	Buy/ Sell	Lots/ Units	Entry Price	Exit Price	Close Date/Time	Pips W/L	Profit/ Loss	New Balance

TRADE SETUP NOTES:

ADDITIONAL NOTES:

Order Date/Time	Pair	Order Ticket #	Buy/ Sell	Lots/ Units	Entry Price	Exit Price	Close Date/Time	Pips W/L	Profit/ Loss	New Balance

TRADE SETUP NOTES:

ADDITIONAL NOTES:

Order Date/Time	Pair	Order Ticket #	Buy/ Sell	Lots/ Units	Entry Price	Exit Price	Close Date/Time	Pips W/L	Profit/ Loss	New Balance

TRADE SETUP NOTES:

ADDITIONAL NOTES:

Order Date/Time	Pair	Order Ticket #	Buy/ Sell	Lots/ Units	Entry Price	Exit Price	Close Date/Time	Pips W/L	Profit/ Loss	New Balance

TRADE SETUP NOTES:

ADDITIONAL NOTES:

Order Date/Time	Pair	Order Ticket #	Buy/ Sell	Lots/ Units	Entry Price	Exit Price	Close Date/Time	Pips W/L	Profit/ Loss	New Balance

TRADE SETUP NOTES:

ADDITIONAL NOTES:

TRADING LOG

Order Date/Time	Pair	Order Ticket #	Buy/ Sell	Lots/ Units	Entry Price	Exit Price	Close Date/Time	Pips W/L	Profit/ Loss	New Balance

TRADE SETUP NOTES:

ADDITIONAL NOTES:

Order Date/Time	Pair	Order Ticket #	Buy/ Sell	Lots/ Units	Entry Price	Exit Price	Close Date/Time	Pips W/L	Profit/ Loss	New Balance

TRADE SETUP NOTES:

ADDITIONAL NOTES:

Order Date/Time	Pair	Order Ticket #	Buy/ Sell	Lots/ Units	Entry Price	Exit Price	Close Date/Time	Pips W/L	Profit/ Loss	New Balance

TRADE SETUP NOTES:

ADDITIONAL NOTES:

Order Date/Time	Pair	Order Ticket #	Buy/ Sell	Lots/ Units	Entry Price	Exit Price	Close Date/Time	Pips W/L	Profit/ Loss	New Balance

TRADE SETUP NOTES:

ADDITIONAL NOTES:

Order Date/Time	Pair	Order Ticket #	Buy/ Sell	Lots/ Units	Entry Price	Exit Price	Close Date/Time	Pips W/L	Profit/ Loss	New Balance

TRADE SETUP NOTES:

ADDITIONAL NOTES:

Order Date/Time	Pair	Order Ticket #	Buy/ Sell	Lots/ Units	Entry Price	Exit Price	Close Date/Time	Pips W/L	Profit/ Loss	New Balance

TRADE SETUP NOTES:

ADDITIONAL NOTES:

Order Date/Time	Pair	Order Ticket #	Buy/ Sell	Lots/ Units	Entry Price	Exit Price	Close Date/Time	Pips W/L	Profit/ Loss	New Balance

TRADE SETUP NOTES:

ADDITIONAL NOTES:

TRADING LOG

Order Date/Time	Pair	Order Ticket #	Buy/ Sell	Lots/ Units	Entry Price	Exit Price	Close Date/Time	Pips W/L	Profit/ Loss	New Balance

TRADE SETUP NOTES:

ADDITIONAl NOTES:

Order Date/Time	Pair	Order Ticket #	Buy/ Sell	Lots/ Units	Entry Price	Exit Price	Close Date/Time	Pips W/L	Profit/ Loss	New Balance

TRADE SETUP NOTES:

ADDITIONAl NOTES:

Order Date/Time	Pair	Order Ticket #	Buy/ Sell	Lots/ Units	Entry Price	Exit Price	Close Date/Time	Pips W/L	Profit/ Loss	New Balance

TRADE SETUP NOTES:

ADDITIONAl NOTES:

Order Date/Time	Pair	Order Ticket #	Buy/ Sell	Lots/ Units	Entry Price	Exit Price	Close Date/Time	Pips W/L	Profit/ Loss	New Balance

TRADE SETUP NOTES:

ADDITIONAl NOTES:

Order Date/Time	Pair	Order Ticket #	Buy/ Sell	Lots/ Units	Entry Price	Exit Price	Close Date/Time	Pips W/L	Profit/ Loss	New Balance

TRADE SETUP NOTES:

ADDITIONAl NOTES:

Order Date/Time	Pair	Order Ticket #	Buy/ Sell	Lots/ Units	Entry Price	Exit Price	Close Date/Time	Pips W/L	Profit/ Loss	New Balance

TRADE SETUP NOTES:

ADDITIONAl NOTES:

TRADING LOG

Order Date/Time	Pair	Order Ticket #	Buy/ Sell	Lots/ Units	Entry Price	Exit Price	Close Date/Time	Pips W/L	Profit/ Loss	New Balance

TRADE SETUP NOTES:

ADDITIONAL NOTES:

Order Date/Time	Pair	Order Ticket #	Buy/ Sell	Lots/ Units	Entry Price	Exit Price	Close Date/Time	Pips W/L	Profit/ Loss	New Balance

TRADE SETUP NOTES:

ADDITIONAL NOTES:

Order Date/Time	Pair	Order Ticket #	Buy/ Sell	Lots/ Units	Entry Price	Exit Price	Close Date/Time	Pips W/L	Profit/ Loss	New Balance

TRADE SETUP NOTES:

ADDITIONAL NOTES:

Order Date/Time	Pair	Order Ticket #	Buy/ Sell	Lots/ Units	Entry Price	Exit Price	Close Date/Time	Pips W/L	Profit/ Loss	New Balance

TRADE SETUP NOTES:

ADDITIONAL NOTES:

Order Date/Time	Pair	Order Ticket #	Buy/ Sell	Lots/ Units	Entry Price	Exit Price	Close Date/Time	Pips W/L	Profit/ Loss	New Balance

TRADE SETUP NOTES:

ADDITIONAL NOTES:

Order Date/Time	Pair	Order Ticket #	Buy/ Sell	Lots/ Units	Entry Price	Exit Price	Close Date/Time	Pips W/L	Profit/ Loss	New Balance

TRADE SETUP NOTES:

ADDITIONAL NOTES:

Order Date/Time	Pair	Order Ticket #	Buy/ Sell	Lots/ Units	Entry Price	Exit Price	Close Date/Time	Pips W/L	Profit/ Loss	New Balance

TRADE SETUP NOTES:

ADDITIONAL NOTES:

TRADING LOG

Order Date/Time	Pair	Order Ticket #	Buy/ Sell	Lots/ Units	Entry Price	Exit Price	Close Date/Time	Pips W/L	Profit/ Loss	New Balance

TRADE SETUP NOTES:

ADDITIONAL NOTES:

Order Date/Time	Pair	Order Ticket #	Buy/ Sell	Lots/ Units	Entry Price	Exit Price	Close Date/Time	Pips W/L	Profit/ Loss	New Balance

TRADE SETUP NOTES:

ADDITIONAL NOTES:

Order Date/Time	Pair	Order Ticket #	Buy/ Sell	Lots/ Units	Entry Price	Exit Price	Close Date/Time	Pips W/L	Profit/ Loss	New Balance

TRADE SETUP NOTES:

ADDITIONAL NOTES:

Order Date/Time	Pair	Order Ticket #	Buy/ Sell	Lots/ Units	Entry Price	Exit Price	Close Date/Time	Pips W/L	Profit/ Loss	New Balance

TRADE SETUP NOTES:

ADDITIONAL NOTES:

Order Date/Time	Pair	Order Ticket #	Buy/ Sell	Lots/ Units	Entry Price	Exit Price	Close Date/Time	Pips W/L	Profit/ Loss	New Balance

TRADE SETUP NOTES:

ADDITIONAL NOTES:

Order Date/Time	Pair	Order Ticket #	Buy/ Sell	Lots/ Units	Entry Price	Exit Price	Close Date/Time	Pips W/L	Profit/ Loss	New Balance

TRADE SETUP NOTES:

ADDITIONAL NOTES:

TRADING LOG

Order Date/Time	Pair	Order Ticket #	Buy/ Sell	Lots/ Units	Entry Price	Exit Price	Close Date/Time	Pips W/L	Profit/ Loss	New Balance

TRADE SETUP NOTES:

ADDITIONAL NOTES:

Order Date/Time	Pair	Order Ticket #	Buy/ Sell	Lots/ Units	Entry Price	Exit Price	Close Date/Time	Pips W/L	Profit/ Loss	New Balance

TRADE SETUP NOTES:

ADDITIONAL NOTES:

Order Date/Time	Pair	Order Ticket #	Buy/ Sell	Lots/ Units	Entry Price	Exit Price	Close Date/Time	Pips W/L	Profit/ Loss	New Balance

TRADE SETUP NOTES:

ADDITIONAL NOTES:

Order Date/Time	Pair	Order Ticket #	Buy/ Sell	Lots/ Units	Entry Price	Exit Price	Close Date/Time	Pips W/L	Profit/ Loss	New Balance

TRADE SETUP NOTES:

ADDITIONAL NOTES:

Order Date/Time	Pair	Order Ticket #	Buy/ Sell	Lots/ Units	Entry Price	Exit Price	Close Date/Time	Pips W/L	Profit/ Loss	New Balance

TRADE SETUP NOTES:

ADDITIONAL NOTES:

Order Date/Time	Pair	Order Ticket #	Buy/ Sell	Lots/ Units	Entry Price	Exit Price	Close Date/Time	Pips W/L	Profit/ Loss	New Balance

TRADE SETUP NOTES:

ADDITIONAL NOTES:

TRADING LOG

Order Date/Time	Pair	Order Ticket #	Buy/ Sell	Lots/ Units	Entry Price	Exit Price	Close Date/Time	Pips W/L	Profit/ Loss	New Balance

TRADE SETUP NOTES:

ADDITIONAl NOTES:

Order Date/Time	Pair	Order Ticket #	Buy/ Sell	Lots/ Units	Entry Price	Exit Price	Close Date/Time	Pips W/L	Profit/ Loss	New Balance

TRADE SETUP NOTES:

ADDITIONAl NOTES:

Order Date/Time	Pair	Order Ticket #	Buy/ Sell	Lots/ Units	Entry Price	Exit Price	Close Date/Time	Pips W/L	Profit/ Loss	New Balance

TRADE SETUP NOTES:

ADDITIONAl NOTES:

Order Date/Time	Pair	Order Ticket #	Buy/ Sell	Lots/ Units	Entry Price	Exit Price	Close Date/Time	Pips W/L	Profit/ Loss	New Balance

TRADE SETUP NOTES:

ADDITIONAl NOTES:

Order Date/Time	Pair	Order Ticket #	Buy/ Sell	Lots/ Units	Entry Price	Exit Price	Close Date/Time	Pips W/L	Profit/ Loss	New Balance

TRADE SETUP NOTES:

ADDITIONAl NOTES:

Order Date/Time	Pair	Order Ticket #	Buy/ Sell	Lots/ Units	Entry Price	Exit Price	Close Date/Time	Pips W/L	Profit/ Loss	New Balance

TRADE SETUP NOTES:

ADDITIONAl NOTES:

TRADING LOG

Order Date/Time	Pair	Order Ticket #	Buy/ Sell	Lots/ Units	Entry Price	Exit Price	Close Date/Time	Pips W/L	Profit/ Loss	New Balance

TRADE SETUP NOTES:

ADDITIONAL NOTES:

Order Date/Time	Pair	Order Ticket #	Buy/ Sell	Lots/ Units	Entry Price	Exit Price	Close Date/Time	Pips W/L	Profit/ Loss	New Balance

TRADE SETUP NOTES:

ADDITIONAL NOTES:

Order Date/Time	Pair	Order Ticket #	Buy/ Sell	Lots/ Units	Entry Price	Exit Price	Close Date/Time	Pips W/L	Profit/ Loss	New Balance

TRADE SETUP NOTES:

ADDITIONAL NOTES:

Order Date/Time	Pair	Order Ticket #	Buy/ Sell	Lots/ Units	Entry Price	Exit Price	Close Date/Time	Pips W/L	Profit/ Loss	New Balance

TRADE SETUP NOTES:

ADDITIONAL NOTES:

Order Date/Time	Pair	Order Ticket #	Buy/ Sell	Lots/ Units	Entry Price	Exit Price	Close Date/Time	Pips W/L	Profit/ Loss	New Balance

TRADE SETUP NOTES:

ADDITIONAL NOTES:

Order Date/Time	Pair	Order Ticket #	Buy/ Sell	Lots/ Units	Entry Price	Exit Price	Close Date/Time	Pips W/L	Profit/ Loss	New Balance

TRADE SETUP NOTES:

ADDITIONAL NOTES:

Order Date/Time	Pair	Order Ticket #	Buy/ Sell	Lots/ Units	Entry Price	Exit Price	Close Date/Time	Pips W/L	Profit/ Loss	New Balance

TRADE SETUP NOTES:

ADDITIONAL NOTES:

TRADING LOG

Order Date/Time	Pair	Order Ticket #	Buy/ Sell	Lots/ Units	Entry Price	Exit Price	Close Date/Time	Pips W/L	Profit/ Loss	New Balance

TRADE SETUP NOTES:

ADDITIONAl NOTES:

Order Date/Time	Pair	Order Ticket #	Buy/ Sell	Lots/ Units	Entry Price	Exit Price	Close Date/Time	Pips W/L	Profit/ Loss	New Balance

TRADE SETUP NOTES:

ADDITIONAl NOTES:

Order Date/Time	Pair	Order Ticket #	Buy/ Sell	Lots/ Units	Entry Price	Exit Price	Close Date/Time	Pips W/L	Profit/ Loss	New Balance

TRADE SETUP NOTES:

ADDITIONAl NOTES:

Order Date/Time	Pair	Order Ticket #	Buy/ Sell	Lots/ Units	Entry Price	Exit Price	Close Date/Time	Pips W/L	Profit/ Loss	New Balance

TRADE SETUP NOTES:

ADDITIONAl NOTES:

Order Date/Time	Pair	Order Ticket #	Buy/ Sell	Lots/ Units	Entry Price	Exit Price	Close Date/Time	Pips W/L	Profit/ Loss	New Balance

TRADE SETUP NOTES:

ADDITIONAl NOTES:

Order Date/Time	Pair	Order Ticket #	Buy/ Sell	Lots/ Units	Entry Price	Exit Price	Close Date/Time	Pips W/L	Profit/ Loss	New Balance

TRADE SETUP NOTES:

ADDITIONAl NOTES:

TRADING LOG

Order Date/Time	Pair	Order Ticket #	Buy/ Sell	Lots/ Units	Entry Price	Exit Price	Close Date/Time	Pips W/L	Profit/ Loss	New Balance

TRADE SETUP NOTES:

ADDITIONAL NOTES:

Order Date/Time	Pair	Order Ticket #	Buy/ Sell	Lots/ Units	Entry Price	Exit Price	Close Date/Time	Pips W/L	Profit/ Loss	New Balance

TRADE SETUP NOTES:

ADDITIONAL NOTES:

Order Date/Time	Pair	Order Ticket #	Buy/ Sell	Lots/ Units	Entry Price	Exit Price	Close Date/Time	Pips W/L	Profit/ Loss	New Balance

TRADE SETUP NOTES:

ADDITIONAL NOTES:

Order Date/Time	Pair	Order Ticket #	Buy/ Sell	Lots/ Units	Entry Price	Exit Price	Close Date/Time	Pips W/L	Profit/ Loss	New Balance

TRADE SETUP NOTES:

ADDITIONAL NOTES:

Order Date/Time	Pair	Order Ticket #	Buy/ Sell	Lots/ Units	Entry Price	Exit Price	Close Date/Time	Pips W/L	Profit/ Loss	New Balance

TRADE SETUP NOTES:

ADDITIONAL NOTES:

Order Date/Time	Pair	Order Ticket #	Buy/ Sell	Lots/ Units	Entry Price	Exit Price	Close Date/Time	Pips W/L	Profit/ Loss	New Balance

TRADE SETUP NOTES:

ADDITIONAL NOTES:

Order Date/Time	Pair	Order Ticket #	Buy/ Sell	Lots/ Units	Entry Price	Exit Price	Close Date/Time	Pips W/L	Profit/ Loss	New Balance

TRADE SETUP NOTES:

ADDITIONAL NOTES:

TRADING LOG

Order Date/Time	Pair	Order Ticket #	Buy/ Sell	Lots/ Units	Entry Price	Exit Price	Close Date/Time	Pips W/L	Profit/ Loss	New Balance

TRADE SETUP NOTES:

ADDITIONAl NOTES:

Order Date/Time	Pair	Order Ticket #	Buy/ Sell	Lots/ Units	Entry Price	Exit Price	Close Date/Time	Pips W/L	Profit/ Loss	New Balance

TRADE SETUP NOTES:

ADDITIONAl NOTES:

Order Date/Time	Pair	Order Ticket #	Buy/ Sell	Lots/ Units	Entry Price	Exit Price	Close Date/Time	Pips W/L	Profit/ Loss	New Balance

TRADE SETUP NOTES:

ADDITIONAl NOTES:

Order Date/Time	Pair	Order Ticket #	Buy/ Sell	Lots/ Units	Entry Price	Exit Price	Close Date/Time	Pips W/L	Profit/ Loss	New Balance

TRADE SETUP NOTES:

ADDITIONAl NOTES:

Order Date/Time	Pair	Order Ticket #	Buy/ Sell	Lots/ Units	Entry Price	Exit Price	Close Date/Time	Pips W/L	Profit/ Loss	New Balance

TRADE SETUP NOTES:

ADDITIONAl NOTES:

Order Date/Time	Pair	Order Ticket #	Buy/ Sell	Lots/ Units	Entry Price	Exit Price	Close Date/Time	Pips W/L	Profit/ Loss	New Balance

TRADE SETUP NOTES:

ADDITIONAl NOTES:

TRADING LOG

Order Date/Time	Pair	Order Ticket #	Buy/ Sell	Lots/ Units	Entry Price	Exit Price	Close Date/Time	Pips W/L	Profit/ Loss	New Balance

TRADE SETUP NOTES:

ADDITIONAl NOTES:

Order Date/Time	Pair	Order Ticket #	Buy/ Sell	Lots/ Units	Entry Price	Exit Price	Close Date/Time	Pips W/L	Profit/ Loss	New Balance

TRADE SETUP NOTES:

ADDITIONAl NOTES:

Order Date/Time	Pair	Order Ticket #	Buy/ Sell	Lots/ Units	Entry Price	Exit Price	Close Date/Time	Pips W/L	Profit/ Loss	New Balance

TRADE SETUP NOTES:

ADDITIONAl NOTES:

Order Date/Time	Pair	Order Ticket #	Buy/ Sell	Lots/ Units	Entry Price	Exit Price	Close Date/Time	Pips W/L	Profit/ Loss	New Balance

TRADE SETUP NOTES:

ADDITIONAl NOTES:

Order Date/Time	Pair	Order Ticket #	Buy/ Sell	Lots/ Units	Entry Price	Exit Price	Close Date/Time	Pips W/L	Profit/ Loss	New Balance

TRADE SETUP NOTES:

ADDITIONAl NOTES:

Order Date/Time	Pair	Order Ticket #	Buy/ Sell	Lots/ Units	Entry Price	Exit Price	Close Date/Time	Pips W/L	Profit/ Loss	New Balance

TRADE SETUP NOTES:

ADDITIONAl NOTES:

Order Date/Time	Pair	Order Ticket #	Buy/ Sell	Lots/ Units	Entry Price	Exit Price	Close Date/Time	Pips W/L	Profit/ Loss	New Balance

TRADE SETUP NOTES:

ADDITIONAl NOTES:

TRADING LOG

Order Date/Time	Pair	Order Ticket #	Buy/ Sell	Lots/ Units	Entry Price	Exit Price	Close Date/Time	Pips W/L	Profit/ Loss	New Balance

TRADE SETUP NOTES:

ADDITIONAl NOTES:

Order Date/Time	Pair	Order Ticket #	Buy/ Sell	Lots/ Units	Entry Price	Exit Price	Close Date/Time	Pips W/L	Profit/ Loss	New Balance

TRADE SETUP NOTES:

ADDITIONAl NOTES:

Order Date/Time	Pair	Order Ticket #	Buy/ Sell	Lots/ Units	Entry Price	Exit Price	Close Date/Time	Pips W/L	Profit/ Loss	New Balance

TRADE SETUP NOTES:

ADDITIONAl NOTES:

Order Date/Time	Pair	Order Ticket #	Buy/ Sell	Lots/ Units	Entry Price	Exit Price	Close Date/Time	Pips W/L	Profit/ Loss	New Balance

TRADE SETUP NOTES:

ADDITIONAl NOTES:

Order Date/Time	Pair	Order Ticket #	Buy/ Sell	Lots/ Units	Entry Price	Exit Price	Close Date/Time	Pips W/L	Profit/ Loss	New Balance

TRADE SETUP NOTES:

ADDITIONAl NOTES:

Order Date/Time	Pair	Order Ticket #	Buy/ Sell	Lots/ Units	Entry Price	Exit Price	Close Date/Time	Pips W/L	Profit/ Loss	New Balance

TRADE SETUP NOTES:

ADDITIONAl NOTES:

TRADING LOG

Order Date/Time	Pair	Order Ticket #	Buy/ Sell	Lots/ Units	Entry Price	Exit Price	Close Date/Time	Pips W/L	Profit/ Loss	New Balance

TRADE SETUP NOTES:

ADDITIONAL NOTES:

Order Date/Time	Pair	Order Ticket #	Buy/ Sell	Lots/ Units	Entry Price	Exit Price	Close Date/Time	Pips W/L	Profit/ Loss	New Balance

TRADE SETUP NOTES:

ADDITIONAL NOTES:

Order Date/Time	Pair	Order Ticket #	Buy/ Sell	Lots/ Units	Entry Price	Exit Price	Close Date/Time	Pips W/L	Profit/ Loss	New Balance

TRADE SETUP NOTES:

ADDITIONAL NOTES:

Order Date/Time	Pair	Order Ticket #	Buy/ Sell	Lots/ Units	Entry Price	Exit Price	Close Date/Time	Pips W/L	Profit/ Loss	New Balance

TRADE SETUP NOTES:

ADDITIONAL NOTES:

Order Date/Time	Pair	Order Ticket #	Buy/ Sell	Lots/ Units	Entry Price	Exit Price	Close Date/Time	Pips W/L	Profit/ Loss	New Balance

TRADE SETUP NOTES:

ADDITIONAL NOTES:

Order Date/Time	Pair	Order Ticket #	Buy/ Sell	Lots/ Units	Entry Price	Exit Price	Close Date/Time	Pips W/L	Profit/ Loss	New Balance

TRADE SETUP NOTES:

ADDITIONAL NOTES:

Order Date/Time	Pair	Order Ticket #	Buy/ Sell	Lots/ Units	Entry Price	Exit Price	Close Date/Time	Pips W/L	Profit/ Loss	New Balance

TRADE SETUP NOTES:

ADDITIONAL NOTES:

TRADING LOG

Order Date/Time	Pair	Order Ticket #	Buy/ Sell	Lots/ Units	Entry Price	Exit Price	Close Date/Time	Pips W/L	Profit/ Loss	New Balance

TRADE SETUP NOTES:

ADDITIONAl NOTES:

Order Date/Time	Pair	Order Ticket #	Buy/ Sell	Lots/ Units	Entry Price	Exit Price	Close Date/Time	Pips W/L	Profit/ Loss	New Balance

TRADE SETUP NOTES:

ADDITIONAl NOTES:

Order Date/Time	Pair	Order Ticket #	Buy/ Sell	Lots/ Units	Entry Price	Exit Price	Close Date/Time	Pips W/L	Profit/ Loss	New Balance

TRADE SETUP NOTES:

ADDITIONAl NOTES:

Order Date/Time	Pair	Order Ticket #	Buy/ Sell	Lots/ Units	Entry Price	Exit Price	Close Date/Time	Pips W/L	Profit/ Loss	New Balance

TRADE SETUP NOTES:

ADDITIONAl NOTES:

Order Date/Time	Pair	Order Ticket #	Buy/ Sell	Lots/ Units	Entry Price	Exit Price	Close Date/Time	Pips W/L	Profit/ Loss	New Balance

TRADE SETUP NOTES:

ADDITIONAl NOTES:

Order Date/Time	Pair	Order Ticket #	Buy/ Sell	Lots/ Units	Entry Price	Exit Price	Close Date/Time	Pips W/L	Profit/ Loss	New Balance

TRADE SETUP NOTES:

ADDITIONAl NOTES:

TRADING LOG

Order Date/Time	Pair	Order Ticket #	Buy/ Sell	Lots/ Units	Entry Price	Exit Price	Close Date/Time	Pips W/L	Profit/ Loss	New Balance

TRADE SETUP NOTES:

ADDITIONAL NOTES:

Order Date/Time	Pair	Order Ticket #	Buy/ Sell	Lots/ Units	Entry Price	Exit Price	Close Date/Time	Pips W/L	Profit/ Loss	New Balance

TRADE SETUP NOTES:

ADDITIONAL NOTES:

Order Date/Time	Pair	Order Ticket #	Buy/ Sell	Lots/ Units	Entry Price	Exit Price	Close Date/Time	Pips W/L	Profit/ Loss	New Balance

TRADE SETUP NOTES:

ADDITIONAL NOTES:

Order Date/Time	Pair	Order Ticket #	Buy/ Sell	Lots/ Units	Entry Price	Exit Price	Close Date/Time	Pips W/L	Profit/ Loss	New Balance

TRADE SETUP NOTES:

ADDITIONAL NOTES:

Order Date/Time	Pair	Order Ticket #	Buy/ Sell	Lots/ Units	Entry Price	Exit Price	Close Date/Time	Pips W/L	Profit/ Loss	New Balance

TRADE SETUP NOTES:

ADDITIONAL NOTES:

Order Date/Time	Pair	Order Ticket #	Buy/ Sell	Lots/ Units	Entry Price	Exit Price	Close Date/Time	Pips W/L	Profit/ Loss	New Balance

TRADE SETUP NOTES:

ADDITIONAL NOTES:

TRADING LOG

Order Date/Time	Pair	Order Ticket #	Buy/ Sell	Lots/ Units	Entry Price	Exit Price	Close Date/Time	Pips W/L	Profit/ Loss	New Balance

TRADE SETUP NOTES:

ADDITIONAL NOTES:

Order Date/Time	Pair	Order Ticket #	Buy/ Sell	Lots/ Units	Entry Price	Exit Price	Close Date/Time	Pips W/L	Profit/ Loss	New Balance

TRADE SETUP NOTES:

ADDITIONAL NOTES:

Order Date/Time	Pair	Order Ticket #	Buy/ Sell	Lots/ Units	Entry Price	Exit Price	Close Date/Time	Pips W/L	Profit/ Loss	New Balance

TRADE SETUP NOTES:

ADDITIONAL NOTES:

Order Date/Time	Pair	Order Ticket #	Buy/ Sell	Lots/ Units	Entry Price	Exit Price	Close Date/Time	Pips W/L	Profit/ Loss	New Balance

TRADE SETUP NOTES:

ADDITIONAL NOTES:

Order Date/Time	Pair	Order Ticket #	Buy/ Sell	Lots/ Units	Entry Price	Exit Price	Close Date/Time	Pips W/L	Profit/ Loss	New Balance

TRADE SETUP NOTES:

ADDITIONAL NOTES:

Order Date/Time	Pair	Order Ticket #	Buy/ Sell	Lots/ Units	Entry Price	Exit Price	Close Date/Time	Pips W/L	Profit/ Loss	New Balance

TRADE SETUP NOTES:

ADDITIONAL NOTES:

TRADING LOG

Order Date/Time	Pair	Order Ticket #	Buy/ Sell	Lots/ Units	Entry Price	Exit Price	Close Date/Time	Pips W/L	Profit/ Loss	New Balance

TRADE SETUP NOTES:

ADDITIONAL NOTES:

Order Date/Time	Pair	Order Ticket #	Buy/ Sell	Lots/ Units	Entry Price	Exit Price	Close Date/Time	Pips W/L	Profit/ Loss	New Balance

TRADE SETUP NOTES:

ADDITIONAL NOTES:

Order Date/Time	Pair	Order Ticket #	Buy/ Sell	Lots/ Units	Entry Price	Exit Price	Close Date/Time	Pips W/L	Profit/ Loss	New Balance

TRADE SETUP NOTES:

ADDITIONAL NOTES:

Order Date/Time	Pair	Order Ticket #	Buy/ Sell	Lots/ Units	Entry Price	Exit Price	Close Date/Time	Pips W/L	Profit/ Loss	New Balance

TRADE SETUP NOTES:

ADDITIONAL NOTES:

Order Date/Time	Pair	Order Ticket #	Buy/ Sell	Lots/ Units	Entry Price	Exit Price	Close Date/Time	Pips W/L	Profit/ Loss	New Balance

TRADE SETUP NOTES:

ADDITIONAL NOTES:

Order Date/Time	Pair	Order Ticket #	Buy/ Sell	Lots/ Units	Entry Price	Exit Price	Close Date/Time	Pips W/L	Profit/ Loss	New Balance

TRADE SETUP NOTES:

ADDITIONAL NOTES:

TRADING LOG

Order Date/Time	Pair	Order Ticket #	Buy/ Sell	Lots/ Units	Entry Price	Exit Price	Close Date/Time	Pips W/L	Profit/ Loss	New Balance

TRADE SETUP NOTES:

ADDITIONAL NOTES:

Order Date/Time	Pair	Order Ticket #	Buy/ Sell	Lots/ Units	Entry Price	Exit Price	Close Date/Time	Pips W/L	Profit/ Loss	New Balance

TRADE SETUP NOTES:

ADDITIONAL NOTES:

Order Date/Time	Pair	Order Ticket #	Buy/ Sell	Lots/ Units	Entry Price	Exit Price	Close Date/Time	Pips W/L	Profit/ Loss	New Balance

TRADE SETUP NOTES:

ADDITIONAL NOTES:

Order Date/Time	Pair	Order Ticket #	Buy/ Sell	Lots/ Units	Entry Price	Exit Price	Close Date/Time	Pips W/L	Profit/ Loss	New Balance

TRADE SETUP NOTES:

ADDITIONAL NOTES:

Order Date/Time	Pair	Order Ticket #	Buy/ Sell	Lots/ Units	Entry Price	Exit Price	Close Date/Time	Pips W/L	Profit/ Loss	New Balance

TRADE SETUP NOTES:

ADDITIONAL NOTES:

Order Date/Time	Pair	Order Ticket #	Buy/ Sell	Lots/ Units	Entry Price	Exit Price	Close Date/Time	Pips W/L	Profit/ Loss	New Balance

TRADE SETUP NOTES:

ADDITIONAL NOTES:

TRADING LOG

Order Date/Time	Pair	Order Ticket #	Buy/ Sell	Lots/ Units	Entry Price	Exit Price	Close Date/Time	Pips W/L	Profit/ Loss	New Balance

TRADE SETUP NOTES:

ADDITIONAL NOTES:

Order Date/Time	Pair	Order Ticket #	Buy/ Sell	Lots/ Units	Entry Price	Exit Price	Close Date/Time	Pips W/L	Profit/ Loss	New Balance

TRADE SETUP NOTES:

ADDITIONAL NOTES:

Order Date/Time	Pair	Order Ticket #	Buy/ Sell	Lots/ Units	Entry Price	Exit Price	Close Date/Time	Pips W/L	Profit/ Loss	New Balance

TRADE SETUP NOTES:

ADDITIONAL NOTES:

Order Date/Time	Pair	Order Ticket #	Buy/ Sell	Lots/ Units	Entry Price	Exit Price	Close Date/Time	Pips W/L	Profit/ Loss	New Balance

TRADE SETUP NOTES:

ADDITIONAL NOTES:

Order Date/Time	Pair	Order Ticket #	Buy/ Sell	Lots/ Units	Entry Price	Exit Price	Close Date/Time	Pips W/L	Profit/ Loss	New Balance

TRADE SETUP NOTES:

ADDITIONAL NOTES:

Order Date/Time	Pair	Order Ticket #	Buy/ Sell	Lots/ Units	Entry Price	Exit Price	Close Date/Time	Pips W/L	Profit/ Loss	New Balance

TRADE SETUP NOTES:

ADDITIONAL NOTES:

Order Date/Time	Pair	Order Ticket #	Buy/ Sell	Lots/ Units	Entry Price	Exit Price	Close Date/Time	Pips W/L	Profit/ Loss	New Balance

TRADE SETUP NOTES:

ADDITIONAL NOTES:

TRADING LOG

Order Date/Time	Pair	Order Ticket #	Buy/ Sell	Lots/ Units	Entry Price	Exit Price	Close Date/Time	Pips W/L	Profit/ Loss	New Balance

TRADE SETUP NOTES:

ADDITIONAL NOTES:

Order Date/Time	Pair	Order Ticket #	Buy/ Sell	Lots/ Units	Entry Price	Exit Price	Close Date/Time	Pips W/L	Profit/ Loss	New Balance

TRADE SETUP NOTES:

ADDITIONAL NOTES:

Order Date/Time	Pair	Order Ticket #	Buy/ Sell	Lots/ Units	Entry Price	Exit Price	Close Date/Time	Pips W/L	Profit/ Loss	New Balance

TRADE SETUP NOTES:

ADDITIONAL NOTES:

Order Date/Time	Pair	Order Ticket #	Buy/ Sell	Lots/ Units	Entry Price	Exit Price	Close Date/Time	Pips W/L	Profit/ Loss	New Balance

TRADE SETUP NOTES:

ADDITIONAL NOTES:

Order Date/Time	Pair	Order Ticket #	Buy/ Sell	Lots/ Units	Entry Price	Exit Price	Close Date/Time	Pips W/L	Profit/ Loss	New Balance

TRADE SETUP NOTES:

ADDITIONAL NOTES:

Order Date/Time	Pair	Order Ticket #	Buy/ Sell	Lots/ Units	Entry Price	Exit Price	Close Date/Time	Pips W/L	Profit/ Loss	New Balance

TRADE SETUP NOTES:

ADDITIONAL NOTES:

TRADING LOG

Order Date/Time	Pair	Order Ticket #	Buy/ Sell	Lots/ Units	Entry Price	Exit Price	Close Date/Time	Pips W/L	Profit/ Loss	New Balance

TRADE SETUP NOTES:

ADDITIONAL NOTES:

Order Date/Time	Pair	Order Ticket #	Buy/ Sell	Lots/ Units	Entry Price	Exit Price	Close Date/Time	Pips W/L	Profit/ Loss	New Balance

TRADE SETUP NOTES:

ADDITIONAL NOTES:

Order Date/Time	Pair	Order Ticket #	Buy/ Sell	Lots/ Units	Entry Price	Exit Price	Close Date/Time	Pips W/L	Profit/ Loss	New Balance

TRADE SETUP NOTES:

ADDITIONAL NOTES:

Order Date/Time	Pair	Order Ticket #	Buy/ Sell	Lots/ Units	Entry Price	Exit Price	Close Date/Time	Pips W/L	Profit/ Loss	New Balance

TRADE SETUP NOTES:

ADDITIONAL NOTES:

Order Date/Time	Pair	Order Ticket #	Buy/ Sell	Lots/ Units	Entry Price	Exit Price	Close Date/Time	Pips W/L	Profit/ Loss	New Balance

TRADE SETUP NOTES:

ADDITIONAL NOTES:

Order Date/Time	Pair	Order Ticket #	Buy/ Sell	Lots/ Units	Entry Price	Exit Price	Close Date/Time	Pips W/L	Profit/ Loss	New Balance

TRADE SETUP NOTES:

ADDITIONAL NOTES:

TRADING LOG

Order Date/Time	Pair	Order Ticket #	Buy/ Sell	Lots/ Units	Entry Price	Exit Price	Close Date/Time	Pips W/L	Profit/ Loss	New Balance

TRADE SETUP NOTES:

ADDITIONAL NOTES:

Order Date/Time	Pair	Order Ticket #	Buy/ Sell	Lots/ Units	Entry Price	Exit Price	Close Date/Time	Pips W/L	Profit/ Loss	New Balance

TRADE SETUP NOTES:

ADDITIONAL NOTES:

Order Date/Time	Pair	Order Ticket #	Buy/ Sell	Lots/ Units	Entry Price	Exit Price	Close Date/Time	Pips W/L	Profit/ Loss	New Balance

TRADE SETUP NOTES:

ADDITIONAL NOTES:

Order Date/Time	Pair	Order Ticket #	Buy/ Sell	Lots/ Units	Entry Price	Exit Price	Close Date/Time	Pips W/L	Profit/ Loss	New Balance

TRADE SETUP NOTES:

ADDITIONAL NOTES:

Order Date/Time	Pair	Order Ticket #	Buy/ Sell	Lots/ Units	Entry Price	Exit Price	Close Date/Time	Pips W/L	Profit/ Loss	New Balance

TRADE SETUP NOTES:

ADDITIONAL NOTES:

Order Date/Time	Pair	Order Ticket #	Buy/ Sell	Lots/ Units	Entry Price	Exit Price	Close Date/Time	Pips W/L	Profit/ Loss	New Balance

TRADE SETUP NOTES:

ADDITIONAL NOTES:

TRADING LOG

Order Date/Time	Pair	Order Ticket #	Buy/ Sell	Lots/ Units	Entry Price	Exit Price	Close Date/Time	Pips W/L	Profit/ Loss	New Balance

TRADE SETUP NOTES:

ADDITIONAL NOTES:

Order Date/Time	Pair	Order Ticket #	Buy/ Sell	Lots/ Units	Entry Price	Exit Price	Close Date/Time	Pips W/L	Profit/ Loss	New Balance

TRADE SETUP NOTES:

ADDITIONAL NOTES:

Order Date/Time	Pair	Order Ticket #	Buy/ Sell	Lots/ Units	Entry Price	Exit Price	Close Date/Time	Pips W/L	Profit/ Loss	New Balance

TRADE SETUP NOTES:

ADDITIONAL NOTES:

Order Date/Time	Pair	Order Ticket #	Buy/ Sell	Lots/ Units	Entry Price	Exit Price	Close Date/Time	Pips W/L	Profit/ Loss	New Balance

TRADE SETUP NOTES:

ADDITIONAL NOTES:

Order Date/Time	Pair	Order Ticket #	Buy/ Sell	Lots/ Units	Entry Price	Exit Price	Close Date/Time	Pips W/L	Profit/ Loss	New Balance

TRADE SETUP NOTES:

ADDITIONAL NOTES:

Order Date/Time	Pair	Order Ticket #	Buy/ Sell	Lots/ Units	Entry Price	Exit Price	Close Date/Time	Pips W/L	Profit/ Loss	New Balance

TRADE SETUP NOTES:

ADDITIONAL NOTES:

TRADING LOG

Order Date/Time	Pair	Order Ticket #	Buy/ Sell	Lots/ Units	Entry Price	Exit Price	Close Date/Time	Pips W/L	Profit/ Loss	New Balance

TRADE SETUP NOTES:

ADDITIONAL NOTES:

Order Date/Time	Pair	Order Ticket #	Buy/ Sell	Lots/ Units	Entry Price	Exit Price	Close Date/Time	Pips W/L	Profit/ Loss	New Balance

TRADE SETUP NOTES:

ADDITIONAL NOTES:

Order Date/Time	Pair	Order Ticket #	Buy/ Sell	Lots/ Units	Entry Price	Exit Price	Close Date/Time	Pips W/L	Profit/ Loss	New Balance

TRADE SETUP NOTES:

ADDITIONAL NOTES:

Order Date/Time	Pair	Order Ticket #	Buy/ Sell	Lots/ Units	Entry Price	Exit Price	Close Date/Time	Pips W/L	Profit/ Loss	New Balance

TRADE SETUP NOTES:

ADDITIONAL NOTES:

Order Date/Time	Pair	Order Ticket #	Buy/ Sell	Lots/ Units	Entry Price	Exit Price	Close Date/Time	Pips W/L	Profit/ Loss	New Balance

TRADE SETUP NOTES:

ADDITIONAL NOTES:

Order Date/Time	Pair	Order Ticket #	Buy/ Sell	Lots/ Units	Entry Price	Exit Price	Close Date/Time	Pips W/L	Profit/ Loss	New Balance

TRADE SETUP NOTES:

ADDITIONAL NOTES:

TRADING LOG

Order Date/Time	Pair	Order Ticket #	Buy/ Sell	Lots/ Units	Entry Price	Exit Price	Close Date/Time	Pips W/L	Profit/ Loss	New Balance

TRADE SETUP NOTES:

ADDITIONAL NOTES:

Order Date/Time	Pair	Order Ticket #	Buy/ Sell	Lots/ Units	Entry Price	Exit Price	Close Date/Time	Pips W/L	Profit/ Loss	New Balance

TRADE SETUP NOTES:

ADDITIONAL NOTES:

Order Date/Time	Pair	Order Ticket #	Buy/ Sell	Lots/ Units	Entry Price	Exit Price	Close Date/Time	Pips W/L	Profit/ Loss	New Balance

TRADE SETUP NOTES:

ADDITIONAL NOTES:

Order Date/Time	Pair	Order Ticket #	Buy/ Sell	Lots/ Units	Entry Price	Exit Price	Close Date/Time	Pips W/L	Profit/ Loss	New Balance

TRADE SETUP NOTES:

ADDITIONAL NOTES:

Order Date/Time	Pair	Order Ticket #	Buy/ Sell	Lots/ Units	Entry Price	Exit Price	Close Date/Time	Pips W/L	Profit/ Loss	New Balance

TRADE SETUP NOTES:

ADDITIONAL NOTES:

Order Date/Time	Pair	Order Ticket #	Buy/ Sell	Lots/ Units	Entry Price	Exit Price	Close Date/Time	Pips W/L	Profit/ Loss	New Balance

TRADE SETUP NOTES:

ADDITIONAL NOTES:

Order Date/Time	Pair	Order Ticket #	Buy/ Sell	Lots/ Units	Entry Price	Exit Price	Close Date/Time	Pips W/L	Profit/ Loss	New Balance

TRADE SETUP NOTES:

ADDITIONAL NOTES:

TRADING LOG

Order Date/Time	Pair	Order Ticket #	Buy/ Sell	Lots/ Units	Entry Price	Exit Price	Close Date/Time	Pips W/L	Profit/ Loss	New Balance

TRADE SETUP NOTES:

ADDITIONAL NOTES:

Order Date/Time	Pair	Order Ticket #	Buy/ Sell	Lots/ Units	Entry Price	Exit Price	Close Date/Time	Pips W/L	Profit/ Loss	New Balance

TRADE SETUP NOTES:

ADDITIONAL NOTES:

Order Date/Time	Pair	Order Ticket #	Buy/ Sell	Lots/ Units	Entry Price	Exit Price	Close Date/Time	Pips W/L	Profit/ Loss	New Balance

TRADE SETUP NOTES:

ADDITIONAL NOTES:

Order Date/Time	Pair	Order Ticket #	Buy/ Sell	Lots/ Units	Entry Price	Exit Price	Close Date/Time	Pips W/L	Profit/ Loss	New Balance

TRADE SETUP NOTES:

ADDITIONAL NOTES:

Order Date/Time	Pair	Order Ticket #	Buy/ Sell	Lots/ Units	Entry Price	Exit Price	Close Date/Time	Pips W/L	Profit/ Loss	New Balance

TRADE SETUP NOTES:

ADDITIONAL NOTES:

Order Date/Time	Pair	Order Ticket #	Buy/ Sell	Lots/ Units	Entry Price	Exit Price	Close Date/Time	Pips W/L	Profit/ Loss	New Balance

TRADE SETUP NOTES:

ADDITIONAL NOTES:

TRADING LOG

Order Date/Time	Pair	Order Ticket #	Buy/ Sell	Lots/ Units	Entry Price	Exit Price	Close Date/Time	Pips W/L	Profit/ Loss	New Balance

TRADE SETUP NOTES:

ADDITIONAL NOTES:

Order Date/Time	Pair	Order Ticket #	Buy/ Sell	Lots/ Units	Entry Price	Exit Price	Close Date/Time	Pips W/L	Profit/ Loss	New Balance

TRADE SETUP NOTES:

ADDITIONAL NOTES:

Order Date/Time	Pair	Order Ticket #	Buy/ Sell	Lots/ Units	Entry Price	Exit Price	Close Date/Time	Pips W/L	Profit/ Loss	New Balance

TRADE SETUP NOTES:

ADDITIONAL NOTES:

Order Date/Time	Pair	Order Ticket #	Buy/ Sell	Lots/ Units	Entry Price	Exit Price	Close Date/Time	Pips W/L	Profit/ Loss	New Balance

TRADE SETUP NOTES:

ADDITIONAL NOTES:

Order Date/Time	Pair	Order Ticket #	Buy/ Sell	Lots/ Units	Entry Price	Exit Price	Close Date/Time	Pips W/L	Profit/ Loss	New Balance

TRADE SETUP NOTES:

ADDITIONAL NOTES:

Order Date/Time	Pair	Order Ticket #	Buy/ Sell	Lots/ Units	Entry Price	Exit Price	Close Date/Time	Pips W/L	Profit/ Loss	New Balance

TRADE SETUP NOTES:

ADDITIONAL NOTES:

Order Date/Time	Pair	Order Ticket #	Buy/ Sell	Lots/ Units	Entry Price	Exit Price	Close Date/Time	Pips W/L	Profit/ Loss	New Balance

TRADE SETUP NOTES:

ADDITIONAL NOTES:

TRADING LOG

Order Date/Time	Pair	Order Ticket #	Buy/ Sell	Lots/ Units	Entry Price	Exit Price	Close Date/Time	Pips W/L	Profit/ Loss	New Balance

TRADE SETUP NOTES:

ADDITIONAl NOTES:

Order Date/Time	Pair	Order Ticket #	Buy/ Sell	Lots/ Units	Entry Price	Exit Price	Close Date/Time	Pips W/L	Profit/ Loss	New Balance

TRADE SETUP NOTES:

ADDITIONAl NOTES:

Order Date/Time	Pair	Order Ticket #	Buy/ Sell	Lots/ Units	Entry Price	Exit Price	Close Date/Time	Pips W/L	Profit/ Loss	New Balance

TRADE SETUP NOTES:

ADDITIONAl NOTES:

Order Date/Time	Pair	Order Ticket #	Buy/ Sell	Lots/ Units	Entry Price	Exit Price	Close Date/Time	Pips W/L	Profit/ Loss	New Balance

TRADE SETUP NOTES:

ADDITIONAl NOTES:

Order Date/Time	Pair	Order Ticket #	Buy/ Sell	Lots/ Units	Entry Price	Exit Price	Close Date/Time	Pips W/L	Profit/ Loss	New Balance

TRADE SETUP NOTES:

ADDITIONAl NOTES:

Order Date/Time	Pair	Order Ticket #	Buy/ Sell	Lots/ Units	Entry Price	Exit Price	Close Date/Time	Pips W/L	Profit/ Loss	New Balance

TRADE SETUP NOTES:

ADDITIONAl NOTES:

TRADING LOG

Order Date/Time	Pair	Order Ticket #	Buy/ Sell	Lots/ Units	Entry Price	Exit Price	Close Date/Time	Pips W/L	Profit/ Loss	New Balance

TRADE SETUP NOTES:

ADDITIONAL NOTES:

Order Date/Time	Pair	Order Ticket #	Buy/ Sell	Lots/ Units	Entry Price	Exit Price	Close Date/Time	Pips W/L	Profit/ Loss	New Balance

TRADE SETUP NOTES:

ADDITIONAL NOTES:

Order Date/Time	Pair	Order Ticket #	Buy/ Sell	Lots/ Units	Entry Price	Exit Price	Close Date/Time	Pips W/L	Profit/ Loss	New Balance

TRADE SETUP NOTES:

ADDITIONAL NOTES:

Order Date/Time	Pair	Order Ticket #	Buy/ Sell	Lots/ Units	Entry Price	Exit Price	Close Date/Time	Pips W/L	Profit/ Loss	New Balance

TRADE SETUP NOTES:

ADDITIONAL NOTES:

Order Date/Time	Pair	Order Ticket #	Buy/ Sell	Lots/ Units	Entry Price	Exit Price	Close Date/Time	Pips W/L	Profit/ Loss	New Balance

TRADE SETUP NOTES:

ADDITIONAL NOTES:

Order Date/Time	Pair	Order Ticket #	Buy/ Sell	Lots/ Units	Entry Price	Exit Price	Close Date/Time	Pips W/L	Profit/ Loss	New Balance

TRADE SETUP NOTES:

ADDITIONAL NOTES:

Order Date/Time	Pair	Order Ticket #	Buy/ Sell	Lots/ Units	Entry Price	Exit Price	Close Date/Time	Pips W/L	Profit/ Loss	New Balance

TRADE SETUP NOTES:

ADDITIONAL NOTES:

TRADING LOG

Order Date/Time	Pair	Order Ticket #	Buy/ Sell	Lots/ Units	Entry Price	Exit Price	Close Date/Time	Pips W/L	Profit/ Loss	New Balance

TRADE SETUP NOTES:

ADDITIONAl NOTES:

Order Date/Time	Pair	Order Ticket #	Buy/ Sell	Lots/ Units	Entry Price	Exit Price	Close Date/Time	Pips W/L	Profit/ Loss	New Balance

TRADE SETUP NOTES:

ADDITIONAl NOTES:

Order Date/Time	Pair	Order Ticket #	Buy/ Sell	Lots/ Units	Entry Price	Exit Price	Close Date/Time	Pips W/L	Profit/ Loss	New Balance

TRADE SETUP NOTES:

ADDITIONAl NOTES:

Order Date/Time	Pair	Order Ticket #	Buy/ Sell	Lots/ Units	Entry Price	Exit Price	Close Date/Time	Pips W/L	Profit/ Loss	New Balance

TRADE SETUP NOTES:

ADDITIONAl NOTES:

Order Date/Time	Pair	Order Ticket #	Buy/ Sell	Lots/ Units	Entry Price	Exit Price	Close Date/Time	Pips W/L	Profit/ Loss	New Balance

TRADE SETUP NOTES:

ADDITIONAl NOTES:

Order Date/Time	Pair	Order Ticket #	Buy/ Sell	Lots/ Units	Entry Price	Exit Price	Close Date/Time	Pips W/L	Profit/ Loss	New Balance

TRADE SETUP NOTES:

ADDITIONAl NOTES:

TRADING LOG

Order Date/Time	Pair	Order Ticket #	Buy/ Sell	Lots/ Units	Entry Price	Exit Price	Close Date/Time	Pips W/L	Profit/ Loss	New Balance

TRADE SETUP NOTES:

ADDITIONAL NOTES:

Order Date/Time	Pair	Order Ticket #	Buy/ Sell	Lots/ Units	Entry Price	Exit Price	Close Date/Time	Pips W/L	Profit/ Loss	New Balance

TRADE SETUP NOTES:

ADDITIONAL NOTES:

Order Date/Time	Pair	Order Ticket #	Buy/ Sell	Lots/ Units	Entry Price	Exit Price	Close Date/Time	Pips W/L	Profit/ Loss	New Balance

TRADE SETUP NOTES:

ADDITIONAL NOTES:

Order Date/Time	Pair	Order Ticket #	Buy/ Sell	Lots/ Units	Entry Price	Exit Price	Close Date/Time	Pips W/L	Profit/ Loss	New Balance

TRADE SETUP NOTES:

ADDITIONAL NOTES:

Order Date/Time	Pair	Order Ticket #	Buy/ Sell	Lots/ Units	Entry Price	Exit Price	Close Date/Time	Pips W/L	Profit/ Loss	New Balance

TRADE SETUP NOTES:

ADDITIONAL NOTES:

Order Date/Time	Pair	Order Ticket #	Buy/ Sell	Lots/ Units	Entry Price	Exit Price	Close Date/Time	Pips W/L	Profit/ Loss	New Balance

TRADE SETUP NOTES:

ADDITIONAL NOTES:

Order Date/Time	Pair	Order Ticket #	Buy/ Sell	Lots/ Units	Entry Price	Exit Price	Close Date/Time	Pips W/L	Profit/ Loss	New Balance

TRADE SETUP NOTES:

ADDITIONAL NOTES:

TRADING LOG

Order Date/Time	Pair	Order Ticket #	Buy/ Sell	Lots/ Units	Entry Price	Exit Price	Close Date/Time	Pips W/L	Profit/ Loss	New Balance

TRADE SETUP NOTES:

ADDITIONAl NOTES:

Order Date/Time	Pair	Order Ticket #	Buy/ Sell	Lots/ Units	Entry Price	Exit Price	Close Date/Time	Pips W/L	Profit/ Loss	New Balance

TRADE SETUP NOTES:

ADDITIONAl NOTES:

Order Date/Time	Pair	Order Ticket #	Buy/ Sell	Lots/ Units	Entry Price	Exit Price	Close Date/Time	Pips W/L	Profit/ Loss	New Balance

TRADE SETUP NOTES:

ADDITIONAl NOTES:

Order Date/Time	Pair	Order Ticket #	Buy/ Sell	Lots/ Units	Entry Price	Exit Price	Close Date/Time	Pips W/L	Profit/ Loss	New Balance

TRADE SETUP NOTES:

ADDITIONAl NOTES:

Order Date/Time	Pair	Order Ticket #	Buy/ Sell	Lots/ Units	Entry Price	Exit Price	Close Date/Time	Pips W/L	Profit/ Loss	New Balance

TRADE SETUP NOTES:

ADDITIONAl NOTES:

Order Date/Time	Pair	Order Ticket #	Buy/ Sell	Lots/ Units	Entry Price	Exit Price	Close Date/Time	Pips W/L	Profit/ Loss	New Balance

TRADE SETUP NOTES:

ADDITIONAl NOTES:

TRADING LOG

Order Date/Time	Pair	Order Ticket #	Buy/ Sell	Lots/ Units	Entry Price	Exit Price	Close Date/Time	Pips W/L	Profit/ Loss	New Balance

TRADE SETUP NOTES:

ADDITIONAL NOTES:

Order Date/Time	Pair	Order Ticket #	Buy/ Sell	Lots/ Units	Entry Price	Exit Price	Close Date/Time	Pips W/L	Profit/ Loss	New Balance

TRADE SETUP NOTES:

ADDITIONAL NOTES:

Order Date/Time	Pair	Order Ticket #	Buy/ Sell	Lots/ Units	Entry Price	Exit Price	Close Date/Time	Pips W/L	Profit/ Loss	New Balance

TRADE SETUP NOTES:

ADDITIONAL NOTES:

Order Date/Time	Pair	Order Ticket #	Buy/ Sell	Lots/ Units	Entry Price	Exit Price	Close Date/Time	Pips W/L	Profit/ Loss	New Balance

TRADE SETUP NOTES:

ADDITIONAL NOTES:

Order Date/Time	Pair	Order Ticket #	Buy/ Sell	Lots/ Units	Entry Price	Exit Price	Close Date/Time	Pips W/L	Profit/ Loss	New Balance

TRADE SETUP NOTES:

ADDITIONAL NOTES:

Order Date/Time	Pair	Order Ticket #	Buy/ Sell	Lots/ Units	Entry Price	Exit Price	Close Date/Time	Pips W/L	Profit/ Loss	New Balance

TRADE SETUP NOTES:

ADDITIONAL NOTES:

TRADING LOG

Order Date/Time	Pair	Order Ticket #	Buy/Sell	Lots/Units	Entry Price	Exit Price	Close Date/Time	Pips W/L	Profit/Loss	New Balance

TRADE SETUP NOTES:

ADDITIONAL NOTES:

Order Date/Time	Pair	Order Ticket #	Buy/Sell	Lots/Units	Entry Price	Exit Price	Close Date/Time	Pips W/L	Profit/Loss	New Balance

TRADE SETUP NOTES:

ADDITIONAL NOTES:

Order Date/Time	Pair	Order Ticket #	Buy/Sell	Lots/Units	Entry Price	Exit Price	Close Date/Time	Pips W/L	Profit/Loss	New Balance

TRADE SETUP NOTES:

ADDITIONAL NOTES:

Order Date/Time	Pair	Order Ticket #	Buy/Sell	Lots/Units	Entry Price	Exit Price	Close Date/Time	Pips W/L	Profit/Loss	New Balance

TRADE SETUP NOTES:

ADDITIONAL NOTES:

Order Date/Time	Pair	Order Ticket #	Buy/Sell	Lots/Units	Entry Price	Exit Price	Close Date/Time	Pips W/L	Profit/Loss	New Balance

TRADE SETUP NOTES:

ADDITIONAL NOTES:

Order Date/Time	Pair	Order Ticket #	Buy/Sell	Lots/Units	Entry Price	Exit Price	Close Date/Time	Pips W/L	Profit/Loss	New Balance

TRADE SETUP NOTES:

ADDITIONAL NOTES:

TRADING LOG

Order Date/Time	Pair	Order Ticket #	Buy/ Sell	Lots/ Units	Entry Price	Exit Price	Close Date/Time	Pips W/L	Profit/ Loss	New Balance

TRADE SETUP NOTES:

ADDITIONAL NOTES:

Order Date/Time	Pair	Order Ticket #	Buy/ Sell	Lots/ Units	Entry Price	Exit Price	Close Date/Time	Pips W/L	Profit/ Loss	New Balance

TRADE SETUP NOTES:

ADDITIONAL NOTES:

Order Date/Time	Pair	Order Ticket #	Buy/ Sell	Lots/ Units	Entry Price	Exit Price	Close Date/Time	Pips W/L	Profit/ Loss	New Balance

TRADE SETUP NOTES:

ADDITIONAL NOTES:

Order Date/Time	Pair	Order Ticket #	Buy/ Sell	Lots/ Units	Entry Price	Exit Price	Close Date/Time	Pips W/L	Profit/ Loss	New Balance

TRADE SETUP NOTES:

ADDITIONAL NOTES:

Order Date/Time	Pair	Order Ticket #	Buy/ Sell	Lots/ Units	Entry Price	Exit Price	Close Date/Time	Pips W/L	Profit/ Loss	New Balance

TRADE SETUP NOTES:

ADDITIONAL NOTES:

Order Date/Time	Pair	Order Ticket #	Buy/ Sell	Lots/ Units	Entry Price	Exit Price	Close Date/Time	Pips W/L	Profit/ Loss	New Balance

TRADE SETUP NOTES:

ADDITIONAL NOTES:

TRADING LOG

Order Date/Time	Pair	Order Ticket #	Buy/ Sell	Lots/ Units	Entry Price	Exit Price	Close Date/Time	Pips W/L	Profit/ Loss	New Balance

TRADE SETUP NOTES:

ADDITIONAl NOTES:

Order Date/Time	Pair	Order Ticket #	Buy/ Sell	Lots/ Units	Entry Price	Exit Price	Close Date/Time	Pips W/L	Profit/ Loss	New Balance

TRADE SETUP NOTES:

ADDITIONAl NOTES:

Order Date/Time	Pair	Order Ticket #	Buy/ Sell	Lots/ Units	Entry Price	Exit Price	Close Date/Time	Pips W/L	Profit/ Loss	New Balance

TRADE SETUP NOTES:

ADDITIONAl NOTES:

Order Date/Time	Pair	Order Ticket #	Buy/ Sell	Lots/ Units	Entry Price	Exit Price	Close Date/Time	Pips W/L	Profit/ Loss	New Balance

TRADE SETUP NOTES:

ADDITIONAl NOTES:

Order Date/Time	Pair	Order Ticket #	Buy/ Sell	Lots/ Units	Entry Price	Exit Price	Close Date/Time	Pips W/L	Profit/ Loss	New Balance

TRADE SETUP NOTES:

ADDITIONAl NOTES:

Order Date/Time	Pair	Order Ticket #	Buy/ Sell	Lots/ Units	Entry Price	Exit Price	Close Date/Time	Pips W/L	Profit/ Loss	New Balance

TRADE SETUP NOTES:

ADDITIONAl NOTES:

TRADING LOG

Order Date/Time	Pair	Order Ticket #	Buy/ Sell	Lots/ Units	Entry Price	Exit Price	Close Date/Time	Pips W/L	Profit/ Loss	New Balance

TRADE SETUP NOTES:

ADDITIONAL NOTES:

Order Date/Time	Pair	Order Ticket #	Buy/ Sell	Lots/ Units	Entry Price	Exit Price	Close Date/Time	Pips W/L	Profit/ Loss	New Balance

TRADE SETUP NOTES:

ADDITIONAL NOTES:

Order Date/Time	Pair	Order Ticket #	Buy/ Sell	Lots/ Units	Entry Price	Exit Price	Close Date/Time	Pips W/L	Profit/ Loss	New Balance

TRADE SETUP NOTES:

ADDITIONAL NOTES:

Order Date/Time	Pair	Order Ticket #	Buy/ Sell	Lots/ Units	Entry Price	Exit Price	Close Date/Time	Pips W/L	Profit/ Loss	New Balance

TRADE SETUP NOTES:

ADDITIONAL NOTES:

Order Date/Time	Pair	Order Ticket #	Buy/ Sell	Lots/ Units	Entry Price	Exit Price	Close Date/Time	Pips W/L	Profit/ Loss	New Balance

TRADE SETUP NOTES:

ADDITIONAL NOTES:

Order Date/Time	Pair	Order Ticket #	Buy/ Sell	Lots/ Units	Entry Price	Exit Price	Close Date/Time	Pips W/L	Profit/ Loss	New Balance

TRADE SETUP NOTES:

ADDITIONAL NOTES:

Order Date/Time	Pair	Order Ticket #	Buy/ Sell	Lots/ Units	Entry Price	Exit Price	Close Date/Time	Pips W/L	Profit/ Loss	New Balance

TRADE SETUP NOTES:

ADDITIONAL NOTES:

TRADING LOG

Order Date/Time	Pair	Order Ticket #	Buy/ Sell	Lots/ Units	Entry Price	Exit Price	Close Date/Time	Pips W/L	Profit/ Loss	New Balance

TRADE SETUP NOTES:

ADDITIONAL NOTES:

Order Date/Time	Pair	Order Ticket #	Buy/ Sell	Lots/ Units	Entry Price	Exit Price	Close Date/Time	Pips W/L	Profit/ Loss	New Balance

TRADE SETUP NOTES:

ADDITIONAL NOTES:

Order Date/Time	Pair	Order Ticket #	Buy/ Sell	Lots/ Units	Entry Price	Exit Price	Close Date/Time	Pips W/L	Profit/ Loss	New Balance

TRADE SETUP NOTES:

ADDITIONAL NOTES:

Order Date/Time	Pair	Order Ticket #	Buy/ Sell	Lots/ Units	Entry Price	Exit Price	Close Date/Time	Pips W/L	Profit/ Loss	New Balance

TRADE SETUP NOTES:

ADDITIONAL NOTES:

Order Date/Time	Pair	Order Ticket #	Buy/ Sell	Lots/ Units	Entry Price	Exit Price	Close Date/Time	Pips W/L	Profit/ Loss	New Balance

TRADE SETUP NOTES:

ADDITIONAL NOTES:

Order Date/Time	Pair	Order Ticket #	Buy/ Sell	Lots/ Units	Entry Price	Exit Price	Close Date/Time	Pips W/L	Profit/ Loss	New Balance

TRADE SETUP NOTES:

ADDITIONAL NOTES:

TRADING LOG

Order Date/Time	Pair	Order Ticket #	Buy/ Sell	Lots/ Units	Entry Price	Exit Price	Close Date/Time	Pips W/L	Profit/ Loss	New Balance

TRADE SETUP NOTES:

ADDITIONAL NOTES:

Order Date/Time	Pair	Order Ticket #	Buy/ Sell	Lots/ Units	Entry Price	Exit Price	Close Date/Time	Pips W/L	Profit/ Loss	New Balance

TRADE SETUP NOTES:

ADDITIONAL NOTES:

Order Date/Time	Pair	Order Ticket #	Buy/ Sell	Lots/ Units	Entry Price	Exit Price	Close Date/Time	Pips W/L	Profit/ Loss	New Balance

TRADE SETUP NOTES:

ADDITIONAL NOTES:

Order Date/Time	Pair	Order Ticket #	Buy/ Sell	Lots/ Units	Entry Price	Exit Price	Close Date/Time	Pips W/L	Profit/ Loss	New Balance

TRADE SETUP NOTES:

ADDITIONAL NOTES:

Order Date/Time	Pair	Order Ticket #	Buy/ Sell	Lots/ Units	Entry Price	Exit Price	Close Date/Time	Pips W/L	Profit/ Loss	New Balance

TRADE SETUP NOTES:

ADDITIONAL NOTES:

Order Date/Time	Pair	Order Ticket #	Buy/ Sell	Lots/ Units	Entry Price	Exit Price	Close Date/Time	Pips W/L	Profit/ Loss	New Balance

TRADE SETUP NOTES:

ADDITIONAL NOTES:

Order Date/Time	Pair	Order Ticket #	Buy/ Sell	Lots/ Units	Entry Price	Exit Price	Close Date/Time	Pips W/L	Profit/ Loss	New Balance

TRADE SETUP NOTES:

ADDITIONAL NOTES:

TRADING LOG

Order Date/Time	Pair	Order Ticket #	Buy/ Sell	Lots/ Units	Entry Price	Exit Price	Close Date/Time	Pips W/L	Profit/ Loss	New Balance

TRADE SETUP NOTES:

ADDITIONAl NOTES:

Order Date/Time	Pair	Order Ticket #	Buy/ Sell	Lots/ Units	Entry Price	Exit Price	Close Date/Time	Pips W/L	Profit/ Loss	New Balance

TRADE SETUP NOTES:

ADDITIONAl NOTES:

Order Date/Time	Pair	Order Ticket #	Buy/ Sell	Lots/ Units	Entry Price	Exit Price	Close Date/Time	Pips W/L	Profit/ Loss	New Balance

TRADE SETUP NOTES:

ADDITIONAl NOTES:

Order Date/Time	Pair	Order Ticket #	Buy/ Sell	Lots/ Units	Entry Price	Exit Price	Close Date/Time	Pips W/L	Profit/ Loss	New Balance

TRADE SETUP NOTES:

ADDITIONAl NOTES:

Order Date/Time	Pair	Order Ticket #	Buy/ Sell	Lots/ Units	Entry Price	Exit Price	Close Date/Time	Pips W/L	Profit/ Loss	New Balance

TRADE SETUP NOTES:

ADDITIONAl NOTES:

Order Date/Time	Pair	Order Ticket #	Buy/ Sell	Lots/ Units	Entry Price	Exit Price	Close Date/Time	Pips W/L	Profit/ Loss	New Balance

TRADE SETUP NOTES:

ADDITIONAl NOTES:

TRADING LOG

Order Date/Time	Pair	Order Ticket #	Buy/ Sell	Lots/ Units	Entry Price	Exit Price	Close Date/Time	Pips W/L	Profit/ Loss	New Balance

TRADE SETUP NOTES:

ADDITIONAL NOTES:

Order Date/Time	Pair	Order Ticket #	Buy/ Sell	Lots/ Units	Entry Price	Exit Price	Close Date/Time	Pips W/L	Profit/ Loss	New Balance

TRADE SETUP NOTES:

ADDITIONAL NOTES:

Order Date/Time	Pair	Order Ticket #	Buy/ Sell	Lots/ Units	Entry Price	Exit Price	Close Date/Time	Pips W/L	Profit/ Loss	New Balance

TRADE SETUP NOTES:

ADDITIONAL NOTES:

Order Date/Time	Pair	Order Ticket #	Buy/ Sell	Lots/ Units	Entry Price	Exit Price	Close Date/Time	Pips W/L	Profit/ Loss	New Balance

TRADE SETUP NOTES:

ADDITIONAL NOTES:

Order Date/Time	Pair	Order Ticket #	Buy/ Sell	Lots/ Units	Entry Price	Exit Price	Close Date/Time	Pips W/L	Profit/ Loss	New Balance

TRADE SETUP NOTES:

ADDITIONAL NOTES:

Order Date/Time	Pair	Order Ticket #	Buy/ Sell	Lots/ Units	Entry Price	Exit Price	Close Date/Time	Pips W/L	Profit/ Loss	New Balance

TRADE SETUP NOTES:

ADDITIONAL NOTES:

Order Date/Time	Pair	Order Ticket #	Buy/ Sell	Lots/ Units	Entry Price	Exit Price	Close Date/Time	Pips W/L	Profit/ Loss	New Balance

TRADE SETUP NOTES:

ADDITIONAL NOTES:

TRADING LOG

Order Date/Time	Pair	Order Ticket #	Buy/ Sell	Lots/ Units	Entry Price	Exit Price	Close Date/Time	Pips W/L	Profit/ Loss	New Balance

TRADE SETUP NOTES:

ADDITIONAL NOTES:

Order Date/Time	Pair	Order Ticket #	Buy/ Sell	Lots/ Units	Entry Price	Exit Price	Close Date/Time	Pips W/L	Profit/ Loss	New Balance

TRADE SETUP NOTES:

ADDITIONAL NOTES:

Order Date/Time	Pair	Order Ticket #	Buy/ Sell	Lots/ Units	Entry Price	Exit Price	Close Date/Time	Pips W/L	Profit/ Loss	New Balance

TRADE SETUP NOTES:

ADDITIONAL NOTES:

Order Date/Time	Pair	Order Ticket #	Buy/ Sell	Lots/ Units	Entry Price	Exit Price	Close Date/Time	Pips W/L	Profit/ Loss	New Balance

TRADE SETUP NOTES:

ADDITIONAL NOTES:

Order Date/Time	Pair	Order Ticket #	Buy/ Sell	Lots/ Units	Entry Price	Exit Price	Close Date/Time	Pips W/L	Profit/ Loss	New Balance

TRADE SETUP NOTES:

ADDITIONAL NOTES:

Order Date/Time	Pair	Order Ticket #	Buy/ Sell	Lots/ Units	Entry Price	Exit Price	Close Date/Time	Pips W/L	Profit/ Loss	New Balance

TRADE SETUP NOTES:

ADDITIONAL NOTES:

TRADING LOG

Order Date/Time	Pair	Order Ticket #	Buy/ Sell	Lots/ Units	Entry Price	Exit Price	Close Date/Time	Pips W/L	Profit/ Loss	New Balance

TRADE SETUP NOTES:

ADDITIONAL NOTES:

Order Date/Time	Pair	Order Ticket #	Buy/ Sell	Lots/ Units	Entry Price	Exit Price	Close Date/Time	Pips W/L	Profit/ Loss	New Balance

TRADE SETUP NOTES:

ADDITIONAL NOTES:

Order Date/Time	Pair	Order Ticket #	Buy/ Sell	Lots/ Units	Entry Price	Exit Price	Close Date/Time	Pips W/L	Profit/ Loss	New Balance

TRADE SETUP NOTES:

ADDITIONAL NOTES:

Order Date/Time	Pair	Order Ticket #	Buy/ Sell	Lots/ Units	Entry Price	Exit Price	Close Date/Time	Pips W/L	Profit/ Loss	New Balance

TRADE SETUP NOTES:

ADDITIONAL NOTES:

Order Date/Time	Pair	Order Ticket #	Buy/ Sell	Lots/ Units	Entry Price	Exit Price	Close Date/Time	Pips W/L	Profit/ Loss	New Balance

TRADE SETUP NOTES:

ADDITIONAL NOTES:

Order Date/Time	Pair	Order Ticket #	Buy/ Sell	Lots/ Units	Entry Price	Exit Price	Close Date/Time	Pips W/L	Profit/ Loss	New Balance

TRADE SETUP NOTES:

ADDITIONAL NOTES:

Order Date/Time	Pair	Order Ticket #	Buy/ Sell	Lots/ Units	Entry Price	Exit Price	Close Date/Time	Pips W/L	Profit/ Loss	New Balance

TRADE SETUP NOTES:

ADDITIONAL NOTES:

TRADING LOG

Order Date/Time	Pair	Order Ticket #	Buy/ Sell	Lots/ Units	Entry Price	Exit Price	Close Date/Time	Pips W/L	Profit/ Loss	New Balance

TRADE SETUP NOTES:

ADDITIONAL NOTES:

Order Date/Time	Pair	Order Ticket #	Buy/ Sell	Lots/ Units	Entry Price	Exit Price	Close Date/Time	Pips W/L	Profit/ Loss	New Balance

TRADE SETUP NOTES:

ADDITIONAL NOTES:

Order Date/Time	Pair	Order Ticket #	Buy/ Sell	Lots/ Units	Entry Price	Exit Price	Close Date/Time	Pips W/L	Profit/ Loss	New Balance

TRADE SETUP NOTES:

ADDITIONAL NOTES:

Order Date/Time	Pair	Order Ticket #	Buy/ Sell	Lots/ Units	Entry Price	Exit Price	Close Date/Time	Pips W/L	Profit/ Loss	New Balance

TRADE SETUP NOTES:

ADDITIONAL NOTES:

Order Date/Time	Pair	Order Ticket #	Buy/ Sell	Lots/ Units	Entry Price	Exit Price	Close Date/Time	Pips W/L	Profit/ Loss	New Balance

TRADE SETUP NOTES:

ADDITIONAL NOTES:

Order Date/Time	Pair	Order Ticket #	Buy/ Sell	Lots/ Units	Entry Price	Exit Price	Close Date/Time	Pips W/L	Profit/ Loss	New Balance

TRADE SETUP NOTES:

ADDITIONAL NOTES:

TRADING LOG

Order Date/Time	Pair	Order Ticket #	Buy/ Sell	Lots/ Units	Entry Price	Exit Price	Close Date/Time	Pips W/L	Profit/ Loss	New Balance

TRADE SETUP NOTES:

ADDITIONAL NOTES:

Order Date/Time	Pair	Order Ticket #	Buy/ Sell	Lots/ Units	Entry Price	Exit Price	Close Date/Time	Pips W/L	Profit/ Loss	New Balance

TRADE SETUP NOTES:

ADDITIONAL NOTES:

Order Date/Time	Pair	Order Ticket #	Buy/ Sell	Lots/ Units	Entry Price	Exit Price	Close Date/Time	Pips W/L	Profit/ Loss	New Balance

TRADE SETUP NOTES:

ADDITIONAL NOTES:

Order Date/Time	Pair	Order Ticket #	Buy/ Sell	Lots/ Units	Entry Price	Exit Price	Close Date/Time	Pips W/L	Profit/ Loss	New Balance

TRADE SETUP NOTES:

ADDITIONAL NOTES:

Order Date/Time	Pair	Order Ticket #	Buy/ Sell	Lots/ Units	Entry Price	Exit Price	Close Date/Time	Pips W/L	Profit/ Loss	New Balance

TRADE SETUP NOTES:

ADDITIONAL NOTES:

Order Date/Time	Pair	Order Ticket #	Buy/ Sell	Lots/ Units	Entry Price	Exit Price	Close Date/Time	Pips W/L	Profit/ Loss	New Balance

TRADE SETUP NOTES:

ADDITIONAL NOTES:

Order Date/Time	Pair	Order Ticket #	Buy/ Sell	Lots/ Units	Entry Price	Exit Price	Close Date/Time	Pips W/L	Profit/ Loss	New Balance

TRADE SETUP NOTES:

ADDITIONAL NOTES:

TRADING LOG

Order Date/Time	Pair	Order Ticket #	Buy/ Sell	Lots/ Units	Entry Price	Exit Price	Close Date/Time	Pips W/L	Profit/ Loss	New Balance

TRADE SETUP NOTES:

ADDITIONAL NOTES:

Order Date/Time	Pair	Order Ticket #	Buy/ Sell	Lots/ Units	Entry Price	Exit Price	Close Date/Time	Pips W/L	Profit/ Loss	New Balance

TRADE SETUP NOTES:

ADDITIONAL NOTES:

Order Date/Time	Pair	Order Ticket #	Buy/ Sell	Lots/ Units	Entry Price	Exit Price	Close Date/Time	Pips W/L	Profit/ Loss	New Balance

TRADE SETUP NOTES:

ADDITIONAL NOTES:

Order Date/Time	Pair	Order Ticket #	Buy/ Sell	Lots/ Units	Entry Price	Exit Price	Close Date/Time	Pips W/L	Profit/ Loss	New Balance

TRADE SETUP NOTES:

ADDITIONAL NOTES:

Order Date/Time	Pair	Order Ticket #	Buy/ Sell	Lots/ Units	Entry Price	Exit Price	Close Date/Time	Pips W/L	Profit/ Loss	New Balance

TRADE SETUP NOTES:

ADDITIONAL NOTES:

Order Date/Time	Pair	Order Ticket #	Buy/ Sell	Lots/ Units	Entry Price	Exit Price	Close Date/Time	Pips W/L	Profit/ Loss	New Balance

TRADE SETUP NOTES:

ADDITIONAL NOTES:

TRADING LOG

Order Date/Time	Pair	Order Ticket #	Buy/ Sell	Lots/ Units	Entry Price	Exit Price	Close Date/Time	Pips W/L	Profit/ Loss	New Balance

TRADE SETUP NOTES:

ADDITIONAL NOTES:

Order Date/Time	Pair	Order Ticket #	Buy/ Sell	Lots/ Units	Entry Price	Exit Price	Close Date/Time	Pips W/L	Profit/ Loss	New Balance

TRADE SETUP NOTES:

ADDITIONAL NOTES:

Order Date/Time	Pair	Order Ticket #	Buy/ Sell	Lots/ Units	Entry Price	Exit Price	Close Date/Time	Pips W/L	Profit/ Loss	New Balance

TRADE SETUP NOTES:

ADDITIONAL NOTES:

Order Date/Time	Pair	Order Ticket #	Buy/ Sell	Lots/ Units	Entry Price	Exit Price	Close Date/Time	Pips W/L	Profit/ Loss	New Balance

TRADE SETUP NOTES:

ADDITIONAL NOTES:

Order Date/Time	Pair	Order Ticket #	Buy/ Sell	Lots/ Units	Entry Price	Exit Price	Close Date/Time	Pips W/L	Profit/ Loss	New Balance

TRADE SETUP NOTES:

ADDITIONAL NOTES:

Order Date/Time	Pair	Order Ticket #	Buy/ Sell	Lots/ Units	Entry Price	Exit Price	Close Date/Time	Pips W/L	Profit/ Loss	New Balance

TRADE SETUP NOTES:

ADDITIONAL NOTES:

Order Date/Time	Pair	Order Ticket #	Buy/ Sell	Lots/ Units	Entry Price	Exit Price	Close Date/Time	Pips W/L	Profit/ Loss	New Balance

TRADE SETUP NOTES:

ADDITIONAL NOTES:

TRADING LOG

Order Date/Time	Pair	Order Ticket #	Buy/ Sell	Lots/ Units	Entry Price	Exit Price	Close Date/Time	Pips W/L	Profit/ Loss	New Balance

TRADE SETUP NOTES:

ADDITIONAl NOTES:

Order Date/Time	Pair	Order Ticket #	Buy/ Sell	Lots/ Units	Entry Price	Exit Price	Close Date/Time	Pips W/L	Profit/ Loss	New Balance

TRADE SETUP NOTES:

ADDITIONAl NOTES:

Order Date/Time	Pair	Order Ticket #	Buy/ Sell	Lots/ Units	Entry Price	Exit Price	Close Date/Time	Pips W/L	Profit/ Loss	New Balance

TRADE SETUP NOTES:

ADDITIONAl NOTES:

Order Date/Time	Pair	Order Ticket #	Buy/ Sell	Lots/ Units	Entry Price	Exit Price	Close Date/Time	Pips W/L	Profit/ Loss	New Balance

TRADE SETUP NOTES:

ADDITIONAl NOTES:

Order Date/Time	Pair	Order Ticket #	Buy/ Sell	Lots/ Units	Entry Price	Exit Price	Close Date/Time	Pips W/L	Profit/ Loss	New Balance

TRADE SETUP NOTES:

ADDITIONAl NOTES:

Order Date/Time	Pair	Order Ticket #	Buy/ Sell	Lots/ Units	Entry Price	Exit Price	Close Date/Time	Pips W/L	Profit/ Loss	New Balance

TRADE SETUP NOTES:

ADDITIONAl NOTES:

TRADING LOG

Order Date/Time	Pair	Order Ticket #	Buy/ Sell	Lots/ Units	Entry Price	Exit Price	Close Date/Time	Pips W/L	Profit/ Loss	New Balance

TRADE SETUP NOTES:

ADDITIONAL NOTES:

Order Date/Time	Pair	Order Ticket #	Buy/ Sell	Lots/ Units	Entry Price	Exit Price	Close Date/Time	Pips W/L	Profit/ Loss	New Balance

TRADE SETUP NOTES:

ADDITIONAL NOTES:

Order Date/Time	Pair	Order Ticket #	Buy/ Sell	Lots/ Units	Entry Price	Exit Price	Close Date/Time	Pips W/L	Profit/ Loss	New Balance

TRADE SETUP NOTES:

ADDITIONAL NOTES:

Order Date/Time	Pair	Order Ticket #	Buy/ Sell	Lots/ Units	Entry Price	Exit Price	Close Date/Time	Pips W/L	Profit/ Loss	New Balance

TRADE SETUP NOTES:

ADDITIONAL NOTES:

Order Date/Time	Pair	Order Ticket #	Buy/ Sell	Lots/ Units	Entry Price	Exit Price	Close Date/Time	Pips W/L	Profit/ Loss	New Balance

TRADE SETUP NOTES:

ADDITIONAL NOTES:

Order Date/Time	Pair	Order Ticket #	Buy/ Sell	Lots/ Units	Entry Price	Exit Price	Close Date/Time	Pips W/L	Profit/ Loss	New Balance

TRADE SETUP NOTES:

ADDITIONAL NOTES:

TRADING LOG

Order Date/Time	Pair	Order Ticket #	Buy/ Sell	Lots/ Units	Entry Price	Exit Price	Close Date/Time	Pips W/L	Profit/ Loss	New Balance

TRADE SETUP NOTES:

ADDITIONAL NOTES:

Order Date/Time	Pair	Order Ticket #	Buy/ Sell	Lots/ Units	Entry Price	Exit Price	Close Date/Time	Pips W/L	Profit/ Loss	New Balance

TRADE SETUP NOTES:

ADDITIONAL NOTES:

Order Date/Time	Pair	Order Ticket #	Buy/ Sell	Lots/ Units	Entry Price	Exit Price	Close Date/Time	Pips W/L	Profit/ Loss	New Balance

TRADE SETUP NOTES:

ADDITIONAL NOTES:

Order Date/Time	Pair	Order Ticket #	Buy/ Sell	Lots/ Units	Entry Price	Exit Price	Close Date/Time	Pips W/L	Profit/ Loss	New Balance

TRADE SETUP NOTES:

ADDITIONAL NOTES:

Order Date/Time	Pair	Order Ticket #	Buy/ Sell	Lots/ Units	Entry Price	Exit Price	Close Date/Time	Pips W/L	Profit/ Loss	New Balance

TRADE SETUP NOTES:

ADDITIONAL NOTES:

Order Date/Time	Pair	Order Ticket #	Buy/ Sell	Lots/ Units	Entry Price	Exit Price	Close Date/Time	Pips W/L	Profit/ Loss	New Balance

TRADE SETUP NOTES:

ADDITIONAL NOTES:

TRADING LOG

Order Date/Time	Pair	Order Ticket #	Buy/ Sell	Lots/ Units	Entry Price	Exit Price	Close Date/Time	Pips W/L	Profit/ Loss	New Balance

TRADE SETUP NOTES:

ADDITIONAL NOTES:

Order Date/Time	Pair	Order Ticket #	Buy/ Sell	Lots/ Units	Entry Price	Exit Price	Close Date/Time	Pips W/L	Profit/ Loss	New Balance

TRADE SETUP NOTES:

ADDITIONAL NOTES:

Order Date/Time	Pair	Order Ticket #	Buy/ Sell	Lots/ Units	Entry Price	Exit Price	Close Date/Time	Pips W/L	Profit/ Loss	New Balance

TRADE SETUP NOTES:

ADDITIONAL NOTES:

Order Date/Time	Pair	Order Ticket #	Buy/ Sell	Lots/ Units	Entry Price	Exit Price	Close Date/Time	Pips W/L	Profit/ Loss	New Balance

TRADE SETUP NOTES:

ADDITIONAL NOTES:

Order Date/Time	Pair	Order Ticket #	Buy/ Sell	Lots/ Units	Entry Price	Exit Price	Close Date/Time	Pips W/L	Profit/ Loss	New Balance

TRADE SETUP NOTES:

ADDITIONAL NOTES:

Order Date/Time	Pair	Order Ticket #	Buy/ Sell	Lots/ Units	Entry Price	Exit Price	Close Date/Time	Pips W/L	Profit/ Loss	New Balance

TRADE SETUP NOTES:

ADDITIONAL NOTES:

Order Date/Time	Pair	Order Ticket #	Buy/ Sell	Lots/ Units	Entry Price	Exit Price	Close Date/Time	Pips W/L	Profit/ Loss	New Balance

TRADE SETUP NOTES:

ADDITIONAL NOTES:

TRADING LOG

Order Date/Time	Pair	Order Ticket #	Buy/ Sell	Lots/ Units	Entry Price	Exit Price	Close Date/Time	Pips W/L	Profit/ Loss	New Balance

TRADE SETUP NOTES:

ADDITIONAL NOTES:

Order Date/Time	Pair	Order Ticket #	Buy/ Sell	Lots/ Units	Entry Price	Exit Price	Close Date/Time	Pips W/L	Profit/ Loss	New Balance

TRADE SETUP NOTES:

ADDITIONAL NOTES:

Order Date/Time	Pair	Order Ticket #	Buy/ Sell	Lots/ Units	Entry Price	Exit Price	Close Date/Time	Pips W/L	Profit/ Loss	New Balance

TRADE SETUP NOTES:

ADDITIONAL NOTES:

Order Date/Time	Pair	Order Ticket #	Buy/ Sell	Lots/ Units	Entry Price	Exit Price	Close Date/Time	Pips W/L	Profit/ Loss	New Balance

TRADE SETUP NOTES:

ADDITIONAL NOTES:

Order Date/Time	Pair	Order Ticket #	Buy/ Sell	Lots/ Units	Entry Price	Exit Price	Close Date/Time	Pips W/L	Profit/ Loss	New Balance

TRADE SETUP NOTES:

ADDITIONAL NOTES:

Order Date/Time	Pair	Order Ticket #	Buy/ Sell	Lots/ Units	Entry Price	Exit Price	Close Date/Time	Pips W/L	Profit/ Loss	New Balance

TRADE SETUP NOTES:

ADDITIONAL NOTES:

TRADING LOG

Order Date/Time	Pair	Order Ticket #	Buy/ Sell	Lots/ Units	Entry Price	Exit Price	Close Date/Time	Pips W/L	Profit/ Loss	New Balance

TRADE SETUP NOTES:

ADDITIONAL NOTES:

Order Date/Time	Pair	Order Ticket #	Buy/ Sell	Lots/ Units	Entry Price	Exit Price	Close Date/Time	Pips W/L	Profit/ Loss	New Balance

TRADE SETUP NOTES:

ADDITIONAL NOTES:

Order Date/Time	Pair	Order Ticket #	Buy/ Sell	Lots/ Units	Entry Price	Exit Price	Close Date/Time	Pips W/L	Profit/ Loss	New Balance

TRADE SETUP NOTES:

ADDITIONAL NOTES:

Order Date/Time	Pair	Order Ticket #	Buy/ Sell	Lots/ Units	Entry Price	Exit Price	Close Date/Time	Pips W/L	Profit/ Loss	New Balance

TRADE SETUP NOTES:

ADDITIONAL NOTES:

Order Date/Time	Pair	Order Ticket #	Buy/ Sell	Lots/ Units	Entry Price	Exit Price	Close Date/Time	Pips W/L	Profit/ Loss	New Balance

TRADE SETUP NOTES:

ADDITIONAL NOTES:

Order Date/Time	Pair	Order Ticket #	Buy/ Sell	Lots/ Units	Entry Price	Exit Price	Close Date/Time	Pips W/L	Profit/ Loss	New Balance

TRADE SETUP NOTES:

ADDITIONAL NOTES:

Order Date/Time	Pair	Order Ticket #	Buy/ Sell	Lots/ Units	Entry Price	Exit Price	Close Date/Time	Pips W/L	Profit/ Loss	New Balance

TRADE SETUP NOTES:

ADDITIONAL NOTES:

TRADING LOG

Order Date/Time	Pair	Order Ticket #	Buy/ Sell	Lots/ Units	Entry Price	Exit Price	Close Date/Time	Pips W/L	Profit/ Loss	New Balance

TRADE SETUP NOTES:

ADDITIONAl NOTES:

Order Date/Time	Pair	Order Ticket #	Buy/ Sell	Lots/ Units	Entry Price	Exit Price	Close Date/Time	Pips W/L	Profit/ Loss	New Balance

TRADE SETUP NOTES:

ADDITIONAl NOTES:

Order Date/Time	Pair	Order Ticket #	Buy/ Sell	Lots/ Units	Entry Price	Exit Price	Close Date/Time	Pips W/L	Profit/ Loss	New Balance

TRADE SETUP NOTES:

ADDITIONAl NOTES:

Order Date/Time	Pair	Order Ticket #	Buy/ Sell	Lots/ Units	Entry Price	Exit Price	Close Date/Time	Pips W/L	Profit/ Loss	New Balance

TRADE SETUP NOTES:

ADDITIONAl NOTES:

Order Date/Time	Pair	Order Ticket #	Buy/ Sell	Lots/ Units	Entry Price	Exit Price	Close Date/Time	Pips W/L	Profit/ Loss	New Balance

TRADE SETUP NOTES:

ADDITIONAl NOTES:

Order Date/Time	Pair	Order Ticket #	Buy/ Sell	Lots/ Units	Entry Price	Exit Price	Close Date/Time	Pips W/L	Profit/ Loss	New Balance

TRADE SETUP NOTES:

ADDITIONAl NOTES:

TRADING LOG

Order Date/Time	Pair	Order Ticket #	Buy/ Sell	Lots/ Units	Entry Price	Exit Price	Close Date/Time	Pips W/L	Profit/ Loss	New Balance

TRADE SETUP NOTES:

ADDITIONAL NOTES:

Order Date/Time	Pair	Order Ticket #	Buy/ Sell	Lots/ Units	Entry Price	Exit Price	Close Date/Time	Pips W/L	Profit/ Loss	New Balance

TRADE SETUP NOTES:

ADDITIONAL NOTES:

Order Date/Time	Pair	Order Ticket #	Buy/ Sell	Lots/ Units	Entry Price	Exit Price	Close Date/Time	Pips W/L	Profit/ Loss	New Balance

TRADE SETUP NOTES:

ADDITIONAL NOTES:

Order Date/Time	Pair	Order Ticket #	Buy/ Sell	Lots/ Units	Entry Price	Exit Price	Close Date/Time	Pips W/L	Profit/ Loss	New Balance

TRADE SETUP NOTES:

ADDITIONAL NOTES:

Order Date/Time	Pair	Order Ticket #	Buy/ Sell	Lots/ Units	Entry Price	Exit Price	Close Date/Time	Pips W/L	Profit/ Loss	New Balance

TRADE SETUP NOTES:

ADDITIONAL NOTES:

Order Date/Time	Pair	Order Ticket #	Buy/ Sell	Lots/ Units	Entry Price	Exit Price	Close Date/Time	Pips W/L	Profit/ Loss	New Balance

TRADE SETUP NOTES:

ADDITIONAL NOTES:

Order Date/Time	Pair	Order Ticket #	Buy/ Sell	Lots/ Units	Entry Price	Exit Price	Close Date/Time	Pips W/L	Profit/ Loss	New Balance

TRADE SETUP NOTES:

ADDITIONAL NOTES:

TRADING LOG

Order Date/Time	Pair	Order Ticket #	Buy/ Sell	Lots/ Units	Entry Price	Exit Price	Close Date/Time	Pips W/L	Profit/ Loss	New Balance

TRADE SETUP NOTES:

ADDITIONAL NOTES:

Order Date/Time	Pair	Order Ticket #	Buy/ Sell	Lots/ Units	Entry Price	Exit Price	Close Date/Time	Pips W/L	Profit/ Loss	New Balance

TRADE SETUP NOTES:

ADDITIONAL NOTES:

Order Date/Time	Pair	Order Ticket #	Buy/ Sell	Lots/ Units	Entry Price	Exit Price	Close Date/Time	Pips W/L	Profit/ Loss	New Balance

TRADE SETUP NOTES:

ADDITIONAL NOTES:

Order Date/Time	Pair	Order Ticket #	Buy/ Sell	Lots/ Units	Entry Price	Exit Price	Close Date/Time	Pips W/L	Profit/ Loss	New Balance

TRADE SETUP NOTES:

ADDITIONAL NOTES:

Order Date/Time	Pair	Order Ticket #	Buy/ Sell	Lots/ Units	Entry Price	Exit Price	Close Date/Time	Pips W/L	Profit/ Loss	New Balance

TRADE SETUP NOTES:

ADDITIONAL NOTES:

Order Date/Time	Pair	Order Ticket #	Buy/ Sell	Lots/ Units	Entry Price	Exit Price	Close Date/Time	Pips W/L	Profit/ Loss	New Balance

TRADE SETUP NOTES:

ADDITIONAL NOTES:

Order Date/Time	Pair	Order Ticket #	Buy/ Sell	Lots/ Units	Entry Price	Exit Price	Close Date/Time	Pips W/L	Profit/ Loss	New Balance

TRADE SETUP NOTES:

ADDITIONAL NOTES:

TRADING LOG

Order Date/Time	Pair	Order Ticket #	Buy/ Sell	Lots/ Units	Entry Price	Exit Price	Close Date/Time	Pips W/L	Profit/ Loss	New Balance

TRADE SETUP NOTES:

ADDITIONAL NOTES:

Order Date/Time	Pair	Order Ticket #	Buy/ Sell	Lots/ Units	Entry Price	Exit Price	Close Date/Time	Pips W/L	Profit/ Loss	New Balance

TRADE SETUP NOTES:

ADDITIONAL NOTES:

Order Date/Time	Pair	Order Ticket #	Buy/ Sell	Lots/ Units	Entry Price	Exit Price	Close Date/Time	Pips W/L	Profit/ Loss	New Balance

TRADE SETUP NOTES:

ADDITIONAL NOTES:

Order Date/Time	Pair	Order Ticket #	Buy/ Sell	Lots/ Units	Entry Price	Exit Price	Close Date/Time	Pips W/L	Profit/ Loss	New Balance

TRADE SETUP NOTES:

ADDITIONAL NOTES:

Order Date/Time	Pair	Order Ticket #	Buy/ Sell	Lots/ Units	Entry Price	Exit Price	Close Date/Time	Pips W/L	Profit/ Loss	New Balance

TRADE SETUP NOTES:

ADDITIONAL NOTES:

Order Date/Time	Pair	Order Ticket #	Buy/ Sell	Lots/ Units	Entry Price	Exit Price	Close Date/Time	Pips W/L	Profit/ Loss	New Balance

TRADE SETUP NOTES:

ADDITIONAL NOTES:

TRADING LOG

Order Date/Time	Pair	Order Ticket #	Buy/ Sell	Lots/ Units	Entry Price	Exit Price	Close Date/Time	Pips W/L	Profit/ Loss	New Balance

TRADE SETUP NOTES:

ADDITIONAL NOTES:

Order Date/Time	Pair	Order Ticket #	Buy/ Sell	Lots/ Units	Entry Price	Exit Price	Close Date/Time	Pips W/L	Profit/ Loss	New Balance

TRADE SETUP NOTES:

ADDITIONAL NOTES:

Order Date/Time	Pair	Order Ticket #	Buy/ Sell	Lots/ Units	Entry Price	Exit Price	Close Date/Time	Pips W/L	Profit/ Loss	New Balance

TRADE SETUP NOTES:

ADDITIONAL NOTES:

Order Date/Time	Pair	Order Ticket #	Buy/ Sell	Lots/ Units	Entry Price	Exit Price	Close Date/Time	Pips W/L	Profit/ Loss	New Balance

TRADE SETUP NOTES:

ADDITIONAL NOTES:

Order Date/Time	Pair	Order Ticket #	Buy/ Sell	Lots/ Units	Entry Price	Exit Price	Close Date/Time	Pips W/L	Profit/ Loss	New Balance

TRADE SETUP NOTES:

ADDITIONAL NOTES:

Order Date/Time	Pair	Order Ticket #	Buy/ Sell	Lots/ Units	Entry Price	Exit Price	Close Date/Time	Pips W/L	Profit/ Loss	New Balance

TRADE SETUP NOTES:

ADDITIONAL NOTES:

TRADING LOG

Order Date/Time	Pair	Order Ticket #	Buy/ Sell	Lots/ Units	Entry Price	Exit Price	Close Date/Time	Pips W/L	Profit/ Loss	New Balance

TRADE SETUP NOTES:

ADDITIONAl NOTES:

Order Date/Time	Pair	Order Ticket #	Buy/ Sell	Lots/ Units	Entry Price	Exit Price	Close Date/Time	Pips W/L	Profit/ Loss	New Balance

TRADE SETUP NOTES:

ADDITIONAl NOTES:

Order Date/Time	Pair	Order Ticket #	Buy/ Sell	Lots/ Units	Entry Price	Exit Price	Close Date/Time	Pips W/L	Profit/ Loss	New Balance

TRADE SETUP NOTES:

ADDITIONAl NOTES:

Order Date/Time	Pair	Order Ticket #	Buy/ Sell	Lots/ Units	Entry Price	Exit Price	Close Date/Time	Pips W/L	Profit/ Loss	New Balance

TRADE SETUP NOTES:

ADDITIONAl NOTES:

Order Date/Time	Pair	Order Ticket #	Buy/ Sell	Lots/ Units	Entry Price	Exit Price	Close Date/Time	Pips W/L	Profit/ Loss	New Balance

TRADE SETUP NOTES:

ADDITIONAl NOTES:

Order Date/Time	Pair	Order Ticket #	Buy/ Sell	Lots/ Units	Entry Price	Exit Price	Close Date/Time	Pips W/L	Profit/ Loss	New Balance

TRADE SETUP NOTES:

ADDITIONAl NOTES:

Order Date/Time	Pair	Order Ticket #	Buy/ Sell	Lots/ Units	Entry Price	Exit Price	Close Date/Time	Pips W/L	Profit/ Loss	New Balance

TRADE SETUP NOTES:

ADDITIONAl NOTES:

TRADING LOG

Order Date/Time	Pair	Order Ticket #	Buy/ Sell	Lots/ Units	Entry Price	Exit Price	Close Date/Time	Pips W/L	Profit/ Loss	New Balance

TRADE SETUP NOTES:

ADDITIONAL NOTES:

Order Date/Time	Pair	Order Ticket #	Buy/ Sell	Lots/ Units	Entry Price	Exit Price	Close Date/Time	Pips W/L	Profit/ Loss	New Balance

TRADE SETUP NOTES:

ADDITIONAL NOTES:

Order Date/Time	Pair	Order Ticket #	Buy/ Sell	Lots/ Units	Entry Price	Exit Price	Close Date/Time	Pips W/L	Profit/ Loss	New Balance

TRADE SETUP NOTES:

ADDITIONAL NOTES:

Order Date/Time	Pair	Order Ticket #	Buy/ Sell	Lots/ Units	Entry Price	Exit Price	Close Date/Time	Pips W/L	Profit/ Loss	New Balance

TRADE SETUP NOTES:

ADDITIONAL NOTES:

Order Date/Time	Pair	Order Ticket #	Buy/ Sell	Lots/ Units	Entry Price	Exit Price	Close Date/Time	Pips W/L	Profit/ Loss	New Balance

TRADE SETUP NOTES:

ADDITIONAL NOTES:

Order Date/Time	Pair	Order Ticket #	Buy/ Sell	Lots/ Units	Entry Price	Exit Price	Close Date/Time	Pips W/L	Profit/ Loss	New Balance

TRADE SETUP NOTES:

ADDITIONAL NOTES:

TRADING LOG

Order Date/Time	Pair	Order Ticket #	Buy/ Sell	Lots/ Units	Entry Price	Exit Price	Close Date/Time	Pips W/L	Profit/ Loss	New Balance

TRADE SETUP NOTES:

ADDITIONAL NOTES:

Order Date/Time	Pair	Order Ticket #	Buy/ Sell	Lots/ Units	Entry Price	Exit Price	Close Date/Time	Pips W/L	Profit/ Loss	New Balance

TRADE SETUP NOTES:

ADDITIONAL NOTES:

Order Date/Time	Pair	Order Ticket #	Buy/ Sell	Lots/ Units	Entry Price	Exit Price	Close Date/Time	Pips W/L	Profit/ Loss	New Balance

TRADE SETUP NOTES:

ADDITIONAL NOTES:

Order Date/Time	Pair	Order Ticket #	Buy/ Sell	Lots/ Units	Entry Price	Exit Price	Close Date/Time	Pips W/L	Profit/ Loss	New Balance

TRADE SETUP NOTES:

ADDITIONAL NOTES:

Order Date/Time	Pair	Order Ticket #	Buy/ Sell	Lots/ Units	Entry Price	Exit Price	Close Date/Time	Pips W/L	Profit/ Loss	New Balance

TRADE SETUP NOTES:

ADDITIONAL NOTES:

Order Date/Time	Pair	Order Ticket #	Buy/ Sell	Lots/ Units	Entry Price	Exit Price	Close Date/Time	Pips W/L	Profit/ Loss	New Balance

TRADE SETUP NOTES:

ADDITIONAL NOTES:

Order Date/Time	Pair	Order Ticket #	Buy/ Sell	Lots/ Units	Entry Price	Exit Price	Close Date/Time	Pips W/L	Profit/ Loss	New Balance

TRADE SETUP NOTES:

ADDITIONAL NOTES:

TRADING LOG

Order Date/Time	Pair	Order Ticket #	Buy/ Sell	Lots/ Units	Entry Price	Exit Price	Close Date/Time	Pips W/L	Profit/ Loss	New Balance

TRADE SETUP NOTES:

ADDITIONAL NOTES:

Order Date/Time	Pair	Order Ticket #	Buy/ Sell	Lots/ Units	Entry Price	Exit Price	Close Date/Time	Pips W/L	Profit/ Loss	New Balance

TRADE SETUP NOTES:

ADDITIONAL NOTES:

Order Date/Time	Pair	Order Ticket #	Buy/ Sell	Lots/ Units	Entry Price	Exit Price	Close Date/Time	Pips W/L	Profit/ Loss	New Balance

TRADE SETUP NOTES:

ADDITIONAL NOTES:

Order Date/Time	Pair	Order Ticket #	Buy/ Sell	Lots/ Units	Entry Price	Exit Price	Close Date/Time	Pips W/L	Profit/ Loss	New Balance

TRADE SETUP NOTES:

ADDITIONAL NOTES:

Order Date/Time	Pair	Order Ticket #	Buy/ Sell	Lots/ Units	Entry Price	Exit Price	Close Date/Time	Pips W/L	Profit/ Loss	New Balance

TRADE SETUP NOTES:

ADDITIONAL NOTES:

Order Date/Time	Pair	Order Ticket #	Buy/ Sell	Lots/ Units	Entry Price	Exit Price	Close Date/Time	Pips W/L	Profit/ Loss	New Balance

TRADE SETUP NOTES:

ADDITIONAL NOTES:

TRADING LOG

Order Date/Time	Pair	Order Ticket #	Buy/ Sell	Lots/ Units	Entry Price	Exit Price	Close Date/Time	Pips W/L	Profit/ Loss	New Balance

TRADE SETUP NOTES:

ADDITIONAl NOTES:

Order Date/Time	Pair	Order Ticket #	Buy/ Sell	Lots/ Units	Entry Price	Exit Price	Close Date/Time	Pips W/L	Profit/ Loss	New Balance

TRADE SETUP NOTES:

ADDITIONAl NOTES:

Order Date/Time	Pair	Order Ticket #	Buy/ Sell	Lots/ Units	Entry Price	Exit Price	Close Date/Time	Pips W/L	Profit/ Loss	New Balance

TRADE SETUP NOTES:

ADDITIONAl NOTES:

Order Date/Time	Pair	Order Ticket #	Buy/ Sell	Lots/ Units	Entry Price	Exit Price	Close Date/Time	Pips W/L	Profit/ Loss	New Balance

TRADE SETUP NOTES:

ADDITIONAl NOTES:

Order Date/Time	Pair	Order Ticket #	Buy/ Sell	Lots/ Units	Entry Price	Exit Price	Close Date/Time	Pips W/L	Profit/ Loss	New Balance

TRADE SETUP NOTES:

ADDITIONAl NOTES:

Order Date/Time	Pair	Order Ticket #	Buy/ Sell	Lots/ Units	Entry Price	Exit Price	Close Date/Time	Pips W/L	Profit/ Loss	New Balance

TRADE SETUP NOTES:

ADDITIONAl NOTES:

Order Date/Time	Pair	Order Ticket #	Buy/ Sell	Lots/ Units	Entry Price	Exit Price	Close Date/Time	Pips W/L	Profit/ Loss	New Balance

TRADE SETUP NOTES:

ADDITIONAl NOTES:

TRADING LOG

Order Date/Time	Pair	Order Ticket #	Buy/ Sell	Lots/ Units	Entry Price	Exit Price	Close Date/Time	Pips W/L	Profit/ Loss	New Balance

TRADE SETUP NOTES:

ADDITIONAL NOTES:

Order Date/Time	Pair	Order Ticket #	Buy/ Sell	Lots/ Units	Entry Price	Exit Price	Close Date/Time	Pips W/L	Profit/ Loss	New Balance

TRADE SETUP NOTES:

ADDITIONAL NOTES:

Order Date/Time	Pair	Order Ticket #	Buy/ Sell	Lots/ Units	Entry Price	Exit Price	Close Date/Time	Pips W/L	Profit/ Loss	New Balance

TRADE SETUP NOTES:

ADDITIONAL NOTES:

Order Date/Time	Pair	Order Ticket #	Buy/ Sell	Lots/ Units	Entry Price	Exit Price	Close Date/Time	Pips W/L	Profit/ Loss	New Balance

TRADE SETUP NOTES:

ADDITIONAL NOTES:

Order Date/Time	Pair	Order Ticket #	Buy/ Sell	Lots/ Units	Entry Price	Exit Price	Close Date/Time	Pips W/L	Profit/ Loss	New Balance

TRADE SETUP NOTES:

ADDITIONAL NOTES:

Order Date/Time	Pair	Order Ticket #	Buy/ Sell	Lots/ Units	Entry Price	Exit Price	Close Date/Time	Pips W/L	Profit/ Loss	New Balance

TRADE SETUP NOTES:

ADDITIONAL NOTES:

TRADING LOG

Order Date/Time	Pair	Order Ticket #	Buy/ Sell	Lots/ Units	Entry Price	Exit Price	Close Date/Time	Pips W/L	Profit/ Loss	New Balance

TRADE SETUP NOTES:

ADDITIONAL NOTES:

Order Date/Time	Pair	Order Ticket #	Buy/ Sell	Lots/ Units	Entry Price	Exit Price	Close Date/Time	Pips W/L	Profit/ Loss	New Balance

TRADE SETUP NOTES:

ADDITIONAL NOTES:

Order Date/Time	Pair	Order Ticket #	Buy/ Sell	Lots/ Units	Entry Price	Exit Price	Close Date/Time	Pips W/L	Profit/ Loss	New Balance

TRADE SETUP NOTES:

ADDITIONAL NOTES:

Order Date/Time	Pair	Order Ticket #	Buy/ Sell	Lots/ Units	Entry Price	Exit Price	Close Date/Time	Pips W/L	Profit/ Loss	New Balance

TRADE SETUP NOTES:

ADDITIONAL NOTES:

Order Date/Time	Pair	Order Ticket #	Buy/ Sell	Lots/ Units	Entry Price	Exit Price	Close Date/Time	Pips W/L	Profit/ Loss	New Balance

TRADE SETUP NOTES:

ADDITIONAL NOTES:

Order Date/Time	Pair	Order Ticket #	Buy/ Sell	Lots/ Units	Entry Price	Exit Price	Close Date/Time	Pips W/L	Profit/ Loss	New Balance

TRADE SETUP NOTES:

ADDITIONAL NOTES:

Order Date/Time	Pair	Order Ticket #	Buy/ Sell	Lots/ Units	Entry Price	Exit Price	Close Date/Time	Pips W/L	Profit/ Loss	New Balance

TRADE SETUP NOTES:

ADDITIONAL NOTES:

TRADING LOG

Order Date/Time	Pair	Order Ticket #	Buy/ Sell	Lots/ Units	Entry Price	Exit Price	Close Date/Time	Pips W/L	Profit/ Loss	New Balance

TRADE SETUP NOTES:

ADDITIONAL NOTES:

Order Date/Time	Pair	Order Ticket #	Buy/ Sell	Lots/ Units	Entry Price	Exit Price	Close Date/Time	Pips W/L	Profit/ Loss	New Balance

TRADE SETUP NOTES:

ADDITIONAL NOTES:

Order Date/Time	Pair	Order Ticket #	Buy/ Sell	Lots/ Units	Entry Price	Exit Price	Close Date/Time	Pips W/L	Profit/ Loss	New Balance

TRADE SETUP NOTES:

ADDITIONAL NOTES:

Order Date/Time	Pair	Order Ticket #	Buy/ Sell	Lots/ Units	Entry Price	Exit Price	Close Date/Time	Pips W/L	Profit/ Loss	New Balance

TRADE SETUP NOTES:

ADDITIONAL NOTES:

Order Date/Time	Pair	Order Ticket #	Buy/ Sell	Lots/ Units	Entry Price	Exit Price	Close Date/Time	Pips W/L	Profit/ Loss	New Balance

TRADE SETUP NOTES:

ADDITIONAL NOTES:

Order Date/Time	Pair	Order Ticket #	Buy/ Sell	Lots/ Units	Entry Price	Exit Price	Close Date/Time	Pips W/L	Profit/ Loss	New Balance

TRADE SETUP NOTES:

ADDITIONAL NOTES:

TRADING LOG

Order Date/Time	Pair	Order Ticket #	Buy/ Sell	Lots/ Units	Entry Price	Exit Price	Close Date/Time	Pips W/L	Profit/ Loss	New Balance

TRADE SETUP NOTES:

ADDITIONAL NOTES:

Order Date/Time	Pair	Order Ticket #	Buy/ Sell	Lots/ Units	Entry Price	Exit Price	Close Date/Time	Pips W/L	Profit/ Loss	New Balance

TRADE SETUP NOTES:

ADDITIONAL NOTES:

Order Date/Time	Pair	Order Ticket #	Buy/ Sell	Lots/ Units	Entry Price	Exit Price	Close Date/Time	Pips W/L	Profit/ Loss	New Balance

TRADE SETUP NOTES:

ADDITIONAL NOTES:

Order Date/Time	Pair	Order Ticket #	Buy/ Sell	Lots/ Units	Entry Price	Exit Price	Close Date/Time	Pips W/L	Profit/ Loss	New Balance

TRADE SETUP NOTES:

ADDITIONAL NOTES:

Order Date/Time	Pair	Order Ticket #	Buy/ Sell	Lots/ Units	Entry Price	Exit Price	Close Date/Time	Pips W/L	Profit/ Loss	New Balance

TRADE SETUP NOTES:

ADDITIONAL NOTES:

Order Date/Time	Pair	Order Ticket #	Buy/ Sell	Lots/ Units	Entry Price	Exit Price	Close Date/Time	Pips W/L	Profit/ Loss	New Balance

TRADE SETUP NOTES:

ADDITIONAL NOTES:

TRADING LOG

Order Date/Time	Pair	Order Ticket #	Buy/ Sell	Lots/ Units	Entry Price	Exit Price	Close Date/Time	Pips W/L	Profit/ Loss	New Balance

TRADE SETUP NOTES:

ADDITIONAL NOTES:

Order Date/Time	Pair	Order Ticket #	Buy/ Sell	Lots/ Units	Entry Price	Exit Price	Close Date/Time	Pips W/L	Profit/ Loss	New Balance

TRADE SETUP NOTES:

ADDITIONAL NOTES:

Order Date/Time	Pair	Order Ticket #	Buy/ Sell	Lots/ Units	Entry Price	Exit Price	Close Date/Time	Pips W/L	Profit/ Loss	New Balance

TRADE SETUP NOTES:

ADDITIONAL NOTES:

Order Date/Time	Pair	Order Ticket #	Buy/ Sell	Lots/ Units	Entry Price	Exit Price	Close Date/Time	Pips W/L	Profit/ Loss	New Balance

TRADE SETUP NOTES:

ADDITIONAL NOTES:

Order Date/Time	Pair	Order Ticket #	Buy/ Sell	Lots/ Units	Entry Price	Exit Price	Close Date/Time	Pips W/L	Profit/ Loss	New Balance

TRADE SETUP NOTES:

ADDITIONAL NOTES:

Order Date/Time	Pair	Order Ticket #	Buy/ Sell	Lots/ Units	Entry Price	Exit Price	Close Date/Time	Pips W/L	Profit/ Loss	New Balance

TRADE SETUP NOTES:

ADDITIONAL NOTES:

TRADING LOG

Order Date/Time	Pair	Order Ticket #	Buy/ Sell	Lots/ Units	Entry Price	Exit Price	Close Date/Time	Pips W/L	Profit/ Loss	New Balance

TRADE SETUP NOTES:

ADDITIONAL NOTES:

Order Date/Time	Pair	Order Ticket #	Buy/ Sell	Lots/ Units	Entry Price	Exit Price	Close Date/Time	Pips W/L	Profit/ Loss	New Balance

TRADE SETUP NOTES:

ADDITIONAL NOTES:

Order Date/Time	Pair	Order Ticket #	Buy/ Sell	Lots/ Units	Entry Price	Exit Price	Close Date/Time	Pips W/L	Profit/ Loss	New Balance

TRADE SETUP NOTES:

ADDITIONAL NOTES:

Order Date/Time	Pair	Order Ticket #	Buy/ Sell	Lots/ Units	Entry Price	Exit Price	Close Date/Time	Pips W/L	Profit/ Loss	New Balance

TRADE SETUP NOTES:

ADDITIONAL NOTES:

Order Date/Time	Pair	Order Ticket #	Buy/ Sell	Lots/ Units	Entry Price	Exit Price	Close Date/Time	Pips W/L	Profit/ Loss	New Balance

TRADE SETUP NOTES:

ADDITIONAL NOTES:

Order Date/Time	Pair	Order Ticket #	Buy/ Sell	Lots/ Units	Entry Price	Exit Price	Close Date/Time	Pips W/L	Profit/ Loss	New Balance

TRADE SETUP NOTES:

ADDITIONAL NOTES:

TRADING LOG

Order Date/Time	Pair	Order Ticket #	Buy/ Sell	Lots/ Units	Entry Price	Exit Price	Close Date/Time	Pips W/L	Profit/ Loss	New Balance

TRADE SETUP NOTES:

ADDITIONAL NOTES:

Order Date/Time	Pair	Order Ticket #	Buy/ Sell	Lots/ Units	Entry Price	Exit Price	Close Date/Time	Pips W/L	Profit/ Loss	New Balance

TRADE SETUP NOTES:

ADDITIONAL NOTES:

Order Date/Time	Pair	Order Ticket #	Buy/ Sell	Lots/ Units	Entry Price	Exit Price	Close Date/Time	Pips W/L	Profit/ Loss	New Balance

TRADE SETUP NOTES:

ADDITIONAL NOTES:

Order Date/Time	Pair	Order Ticket #	Buy/ Sell	Lots/ Units	Entry Price	Exit Price	Close Date/Time	Pips W/L	Profit/ Loss	New Balance

TRADE SETUP NOTES:

ADDITIONAL NOTES:

Order Date/Time	Pair	Order Ticket #	Buy/ Sell	Lots/ Units	Entry Price	Exit Price	Close Date/Time	Pips W/L	Profit/ Loss	New Balance

TRADE SETUP NOTES:

ADDITIONAL NOTES:

Order Date/Time	Pair	Order Ticket #	Buy/ Sell	Lots/ Units	Entry Price	Exit Price	Close Date/Time	Pips W/L	Profit/ Loss	New Balance

TRADE SETUP NOTES:

ADDITIONAL NOTES:

TRADING LOG

Order Date/Time	Pair	Order Ticket #	Buy/ Sell	Lots/ Units	Entry Price	Exit Price	Close Date/Time	Pips W/L	Profit/ Loss	New Balance

TRADE SETUP NOTES:

ADDITIONAL NOTES:

Order Date/Time	Pair	Order Ticket #	Buy/ Sell	Lots/ Units	Entry Price	Exit Price	Close Date/Time	Pips W/L	Profit/ Loss	New Balance

TRADE SETUP NOTES:

ADDITIONAL NOTES:

Order Date/Time	Pair	Order Ticket #	Buy/ Sell	Lots/ Units	Entry Price	Exit Price	Close Date/Time	Pips W/L	Profit/ Loss	New Balance

TRADE SETUP NOTES:

ADDITIONAL NOTES:

Order Date/Time	Pair	Order Ticket #	Buy/ Sell	Lots/ Units	Entry Price	Exit Price	Close Date/Time	Pips W/L	Profit/ Loss	New Balance

TRADE SETUP NOTES:

ADDITIONAL NOTES:

Order Date/Time	Pair	Order Ticket #	Buy/ Sell	Lots/ Units	Entry Price	Exit Price	Close Date/Time	Pips W/L	Profit/ Loss	New Balance

TRADE SETUP NOTES:

ADDITIONAL NOTES:

Order Date/Time	Pair	Order Ticket #	Buy/ Sell	Lots/ Units	Entry Price	Exit Price	Close Date/Time	Pips W/L	Profit/ Loss	New Balance

TRADE SETUP NOTES:

ADDITIONAL NOTES:

TRADING LOG

Order Date/Time	Pair	Order Ticket #	Buy/ Sell	Lots/ Units	Entry Price	Exit Price	Close Date/Time	Pips W/L	Profit/ Loss	New Balance

TRADE SETUP NOTES:

ADDITIONAL NOTES:

Order Date/Time	Pair	Order Ticket #	Buy/ Sell	Lots/ Units	Entry Price	Exit Price	Close Date/Time	Pips W/L	Profit/ Loss	New Balance

TRADE SETUP NOTES:

ADDITIONAL NOTES:

Order Date/Time	Pair	Order Ticket #	Buy/ Sell	Lots/ Units	Entry Price	Exit Price	Close Date/Time	Pips W/L	Profit/ Loss	New Balance

TRADE SETUP NOTES:

ADDITIONAL NOTES:

Order Date/Time	Pair	Order Ticket #	Buy/ Sell	Lots/ Units	Entry Price	Exit Price	Close Date/Time	Pips W/L	Profit/ Loss	New Balance

TRADE SETUP NOTES:

ADDITIONAL NOTES:

Order Date/Time	Pair	Order Ticket #	Buy/ Sell	Lots/ Units	Entry Price	Exit Price	Close Date/Time	Pips W/L	Profit/ Loss	New Balance

TRADE SETUP NOTES:

ADDITIONAL NOTES:

Order Date/Time	Pair	Order Ticket #	Buy/ Sell	Lots/ Units	Entry Price	Exit Price	Close Date/Time	Pips W/L	Profit/ Loss	New Balance

TRADE SETUP NOTES:

ADDITIONAL NOTES:

TRADING LOG

Order Date/Time	Pair	Order Ticket #	Buy/ Sell	Lots/ Units	Entry Price	Exit Price	Close Date/Time	Pips W/L	Profit/ Loss	New Balance

TRADE SETUP NOTES:

ADDITIONAL NOTES:

Order Date/Time	Pair	Order Ticket #	Buy/ Sell	Lots/ Units	Entry Price	Exit Price	Close Date/Time	Pips W/L	Profit/ Loss	New Balance

TRADE SETUP NOTES:

ADDITIONAL NOTES:

Order Date/Time	Pair	Order Ticket #	Buy/ Sell	Lots/ Units	Entry Price	Exit Price	Close Date/Time	Pips W/L	Profit/ Loss	New Balance

TRADE SETUP NOTES:

ADDITIONAL NOTES:

Order Date/Time	Pair	Order Ticket #	Buy/ Sell	Lots/ Units	Entry Price	Exit Price	Close Date/Time	Pips W/L	Profit/ Loss	New Balance

TRADE SETUP NOTES:

ADDITIONAL NOTES:

Order Date/Time	Pair	Order Ticket #	Buy/ Sell	Lots/ Units	Entry Price	Exit Price	Close Date/Time	Pips W/L	Profit/ Loss	New Balance

TRADE SETUP NOTES:

ADDITIONAL NOTES:

Order Date/Time	Pair	Order Ticket #	Buy/ Sell	Lots/ Units	Entry Price	Exit Price	Close Date/Time	Pips W/L	Profit/ Loss	New Balance

TRADE SETUP NOTES:

ADDITIONAL NOTES:

TRADING LOG

Order Date/Time	Pair	Order Ticket #	Buy/ Sell	Lots/ Units	Entry Price	Exit Price	Close Date/Time	Pips W/L	Profit/ Loss	New Balance

TRADE SETUP NOTES:

ADDITIONAL NOTES:

Order Date/Time	Pair	Order Ticket #	Buy/ Sell	Lots/ Units	Entry Price	Exit Price	Close Date/Time	Pips W/L	Profit/ Loss	New Balance

TRADE SETUP NOTES:

ADDITIONAL NOTES:

Order Date/Time	Pair	Order Ticket #	Buy/ Sell	Lots/ Units	Entry Price	Exit Price	Close Date/Time	Pips W/L	Profit/ Loss	New Balance

TRADE SETUP NOTES:

ADDITIONAL NOTES:

Order Date/Time	Pair	Order Ticket #	Buy/ Sell	Lots/ Units	Entry Price	Exit Price	Close Date/Time	Pips W/L	Profit/ Loss	New Balance

TRADE SETUP NOTES:

ADDITIONAL NOTES:

Order Date/Time	Pair	Order Ticket #	Buy/ Sell	Lots/ Units	Entry Price	Exit Price	Close Date/Time	Pips W/L	Profit/ Loss	New Balance

TRADE SETUP NOTES:

ADDITIONAL NOTES:

Order Date/Time	Pair	Order Ticket #	Buy/ Sell	Lots/ Units	Entry Price	Exit Price	Close Date/Time	Pips W/L	Profit/ Loss	New Balance

TRADE SETUP NOTES:

ADDITIONAL NOTES:

TRADING LOG

Order Date/Time	Pair	Order Ticket #	Buy/ Sell	Lots/ Units	Entry Price	Exit Price	Close Date/Time	Pips W/L	Profit/ Loss	New Balance

TRADE SETUP NOTES:

ADDITIONAL NOTES:

Order Date/Time	Pair	Order Ticket #	Buy/ Sell	Lots/ Units	Entry Price	Exit Price	Close Date/Time	Pips W/L	Profit/ Loss	New Balance

TRADE SETUP NOTES:

ADDITIONAL NOTES:

Order Date/Time	Pair	Order Ticket #	Buy/ Sell	Lots/ Units	Entry Price	Exit Price	Close Date/Time	Pips W/L	Profit/ Loss	New Balance

TRADE SETUP NOTES:

ADDITIONAL NOTES:

Order Date/Time	Pair	Order Ticket #	Buy/ Sell	Lots/ Units	Entry Price	Exit Price	Close Date/Time	Pips W/L	Profit/ Loss	New Balance

TRADE SETUP NOTES:

ADDITIONAL NOTES:

Order Date/Time	Pair	Order Ticket #	Buy/ Sell	Lots/ Units	Entry Price	Exit Price	Close Date/Time	Pips W/L	Profit/ Loss	New Balance

TRADE SETUP NOTES:

ADDITIONAL NOTES:

Order Date/Time	Pair	Order Ticket #	Buy/ Sell	Lots/ Units	Entry Price	Exit Price	Close Date/Time	Pips W/L	Profit/ Loss	New Balance

TRADE SETUP NOTES:

ADDITIONAL NOTES:

Order Date/Time	Pair	Order Ticket #	Buy/ Sell	Lots/ Units	Entry Price	Exit Price	Close Date/Time	Pips W/L	Profit/ Loss	New Balance

TRADE SETUP NOTES:

ADDITIONAL NOTES:

TRADING LOG

Order Date/Time	Pair	Order Ticket #	Buy/ Sell	Lots/ Units	Entry Price	Exit Price	Close Date/Time	Pips W/L	Profit/ Loss	New Balance

TRADE SETUP NOTES:

ADDITIONAL NOTES:

Order Date/Time	Pair	Order Ticket #	Buy/ Sell	Lots/ Units	Entry Price	Exit Price	Close Date/Time	Pips W/L	Profit/ Loss	New Balance

TRADE SETUP NOTES:

ADDITIONAL NOTES:

Order Date/Time	Pair	Order Ticket #	Buy/ Sell	Lots/ Units	Entry Price	Exit Price	Close Date/Time	Pips W/L	Profit/ Loss	New Balance

TRADE SETUP NOTES:

ADDITIONAL NOTES:

Order Date/Time	Pair	Order Ticket #	Buy/ Sell	Lots/ Units	Entry Price	Exit Price	Close Date/Time	Pips W/L	Profit/ Loss	New Balance

TRADE SETUP NOTES:

ADDITIONAL NOTES:

Order Date/Time	Pair	Order Ticket #	Buy/ Sell	Lots/ Units	Entry Price	Exit Price	Close Date/Time	Pips W/L	Profit/ Loss	New Balance

TRADE SETUP NOTES:

ADDITIONAL NOTES:

Order Date/Time	Pair	Order Ticket #	Buy/ Sell	Lots/ Units	Entry Price	Exit Price	Close Date/Time	Pips W/L	Profit/ Loss	New Balance

TRADE SETUP NOTES:

ADDITIONAL NOTES:

TRADING LOG

Order Date/Time	Pair	Order Ticket #	Buy/ Sell	Lots/ Units	Entry Price	Exit Price	Close Date/Time	Pips W/L	Profit/ Loss	New Balance

TRADE SETUP NOTES:

ADDITIONAL NOTES:

Order Date/Time	Pair	Order Ticket #	Buy/ Sell	Lots/ Units	Entry Price	Exit Price	Close Date/Time	Pips W/L	Profit/ Loss	New Balance

TRADE SETUP NOTES:

ADDITIONAL NOTES:

Order Date/Time	Pair	Order Ticket #	Buy/ Sell	Lots/ Units	Entry Price	Exit Price	Close Date/Time	Pips W/L	Profit/ Loss	New Balance

TRADE SETUP NOTES:

ADDITIONAL NOTES:

Order Date/Time	Pair	Order Ticket #	Buy/ Sell	Lots/ Units	Entry Price	Exit Price	Close Date/Time	Pips W/L	Profit/ Loss	New Balance

TRADE SETUP NOTES:

ADDITIONAL NOTES:

Order Date/Time	Pair	Order Ticket #	Buy/ Sell	Lots/ Units	Entry Price	Exit Price	Close Date/Time	Pips W/L	Profit/ Loss	New Balance

TRADE SETUP NOTES:

ADDITIONAL NOTES:

Order Date/Time	Pair	Order Ticket #	Buy/ Sell	Lots/ Units	Entry Price	Exit Price	Close Date/Time	Pips W/L	Profit/ Loss	New Balance

TRADE SETUP NOTES:

ADDITIONAL NOTES:

Order Date/Time	Pair	Order Ticket #	Buy/ Sell	Lots/ Units	Entry Price	Exit Price	Close Date/Time	Pips W/L	Profit/ Loss	New Balance

TRADE SETUP NOTES:

ADDITIONAL NOTES:

TRADING LOG

Order Date/Time	Pair	Order Ticket #	Buy/ Sell	Lots/ Units	Entry Price	Exit Price	Close Date/Time	Pips W/L	Profit/ Loss	New Balance

TRADE SETUP NOTES:

ADDITIONAL NOTES:

Order Date/Time	Pair	Order Ticket #	Buy/ Sell	Lots/ Units	Entry Price	Exit Price	Close Date/Time	Pips W/L	Profit/ Loss	New Balance

TRADE SETUP NOTES:

ADDITIONAL NOTES:

Order Date/Time	Pair	Order Ticket #	Buy/ Sell	Lots/ Units	Entry Price	Exit Price	Close Date/Time	Pips W/L	Profit/ Loss	New Balance

TRADE SETUP NOTES:

ADDITIONAL NOTES:

Order Date/Time	Pair	Order Ticket #	Buy/ Sell	Lots/ Units	Entry Price	Exit Price	Close Date/Time	Pips W/L	Profit/ Loss	New Balance

TRADE SETUP NOTES:

ADDITIONAL NOTES:

Order Date/Time	Pair	Order Ticket #	Buy/ Sell	Lots/ Units	Entry Price	Exit Price	Close Date/Time	Pips W/L	Profit/ Loss	New Balance

TRADE SETUP NOTES:

ADDITIONAL NOTES:

Order Date/Time	Pair	Order Ticket #	Buy/ Sell	Lots/ Units	Entry Price	Exit Price	Close Date/Time	Pips W/L	Profit/ Loss	New Balance

TRADE SETUP NOTES:

ADDITIONAL NOTES:

TRADING LOG

Order Date/Time	Pair	Order Ticket #	Buy/ Sell	Lots/ Units	Entry Price	Exit Price	Close Date/Time	Pips W/L	Profit/ Loss	New Balance

TRADE SETUP NOTES:

ADDITIONAL NOTES:

Order Date/Time	Pair	Order Ticket #	Buy/ Sell	Lots/ Units	Entry Price	Exit Price	Close Date/Time	Pips W/L	Profit/ Loss	New Balance

TRADE SETUP NOTES:

ADDITIONAL NOTES:

Order Date/Time	Pair	Order Ticket #	Buy/ Sell	Lots/ Units	Entry Price	Exit Price	Close Date/Time	Pips W/L	Profit/ Loss	New Balance

TRADE SETUP NOTES:

ADDITIONAL NOTES:

Order Date/Time	Pair	Order Ticket #	Buy/ Sell	Lots/ Units	Entry Price	Exit Price	Close Date/Time	Pips W/L	Profit/ Loss	New Balance

TRADE SETUP NOTES:

ADDITIONAL NOTES:

Order Date/Time	Pair	Order Ticket #	Buy/ Sell	Lots/ Units	Entry Price	Exit Price	Close Date/Time	Pips W/L	Profit/ Loss	New Balance

TRADE SETUP NOTES:

ADDITIONAL NOTES:

Order Date/Time	Pair	Order Ticket #	Buy/ Sell	Lots/ Units	Entry Price	Exit Price	Close Date/Time	Pips W/L	Profit/ Loss	New Balance

TRADE SETUP NOTES:

ADDITIONAL NOTES:

Order Date/Time	Pair	Order Ticket #	Buy/ Sell	Lots/ Units	Entry Price	Exit Price	Close Date/Time	Pips W/L	Profit/ Loss	New Balance

TRADE SETUP NOTES:

ADDITIONAL NOTES:

TRADING LOG

Order Date/Time	Pair	Order Ticket #	Buy/ Sell	Lots/ Units	Entry Price	Exit Price	Close Date/Time	Pips W/L	Profit/ Loss	New Balance

TRADE SETUP NOTES:

ADDITIONAL NOTES:

Order Date/Time	Pair	Order Ticket #	Buy/ Sell	Lots/ Units	Entry Price	Exit Price	Close Date/Time	Pips W/L	Profit/ Loss	New Balance

TRADE SETUP NOTES:

ADDITIONAL NOTES:

Order Date/Time	Pair	Order Ticket #	Buy/ Sell	Lots/ Units	Entry Price	Exit Price	Close Date/Time	Pips W/L	Profit/ Loss	New Balance

TRADE SETUP NOTES:

ADDITIONAL NOTES:

Order Date/Time	Pair	Order Ticket #	Buy/ Sell	Lots/ Units	Entry Price	Exit Price	Close Date/Time	Pips W/L	Profit/ Loss	New Balance

TRADE SETUP NOTES:

ADDITIONAL NOTES:

Order Date/Time	Pair	Order Ticket #	Buy/ Sell	Lots/ Units	Entry Price	Exit Price	Close Date/Time	Pips W/L	Profit/ Loss	New Balance

TRADE SETUP NOTES:

ADDITIONAL NOTES:

Order Date/Time	Pair	Order Ticket #	Buy/ Sell	Lots/ Units	Entry Price	Exit Price	Close Date/Time	Pips W/L	Profit/ Loss	New Balance

TRADE SETUP NOTES:

ADDITIONAL NOTES:

TRADING LOG

Order Date/Time	Pair	Order Ticket #	Buy/ Sell	Lots/ Units	Entry Price	Exit Price	Close Date/Time	Pips W/L	Profit/ Loss	New Balance

TRADE SETUP NOTES:

ADDITIONAL NOTES:

Order Date/Time	Pair	Order Ticket #	Buy/ Sell	Lots/ Units	Entry Price	Exit Price	Close Date/Time	Pips W/L	Profit/ Loss	New Balance

TRADE SETUP NOTES:

ADDITIONAL NOTES:

Order Date/Time	Pair	Order Ticket #	Buy/ Sell	Lots/ Units	Entry Price	Exit Price	Close Date/Time	Pips W/L	Profit/ Loss	New Balance

TRADE SETUP NOTES:

ADDITIONAL NOTES:

Order Date/Time	Pair	Order Ticket #	Buy/ Sell	Lots/ Units	Entry Price	Exit Price	Close Date/Time	Pips W/L	Profit/ Loss	New Balance

TRADE SETUP NOTES:

ADDITIONAL NOTES:

Order Date/Time	Pair	Order Ticket #	Buy/ Sell	Lots/ Units	Entry Price	Exit Price	Close Date/Time	Pips W/L	Profit/ Loss	New Balance

TRADE SETUP NOTES:

ADDITIONAL NOTES:

Order Date/Time	Pair	Order Ticket #	Buy/ Sell	Lots/ Units	Entry Price	Exit Price	Close Date/Time	Pips W/L	Profit/ Loss	New Balance

TRADE SETUP NOTES:

ADDITIONAL NOTES:

Order Date/Time	Pair	Order Ticket #	Buy/ Sell	Lots/ Units	Entry Price	Exit Price	Close Date/Time	Pips W/L	Profit/ Loss	New Balance

TRADE SETUP NOTES:

ADDITIONAL NOTES:

TRADING LOG

Order Date/Time	Pair	Order Ticket #	Buy/ Sell	Lots/ Units	Entry Price	Exit Price	Close Date/Time	Pips W/L	Profit/ Loss	New Balance

TRADE SETUP NOTES:

ADDITIONAL NOTES:

Order Date/Time	Pair	Order Ticket #	Buy/ Sell	Lots/ Units	Entry Price	Exit Price	Close Date/Time	Pips W/L	Profit/ Loss	New Balance

TRADE SETUP NOTES:

ADDITIONAL NOTES:

Order Date/Time	Pair	Order Ticket #	Buy/ Sell	Lots/ Units	Entry Price	Exit Price	Close Date/Time	Pips W/L	Profit/ Loss	New Balance

TRADE SETUP NOTES:

ADDITIONAL NOTES:

Order Date/Time	Pair	Order Ticket #	Buy/ Sell	Lots/ Units	Entry Price	Exit Price	Close Date/Time	Pips W/L	Profit/ Loss	New Balance

TRADE SETUP NOTES:

ADDITIONAL NOTES:

Order Date/Time	Pair	Order Ticket #	Buy/ Sell	Lots/ Units	Entry Price	Exit Price	Close Date/Time	Pips W/L	Profit/ Loss	New Balance

TRADE SETUP NOTES:

ADDITIONAL NOTES:

Order Date/Time	Pair	Order Ticket #	Buy/ Sell	Lots/ Units	Entry Price	Exit Price	Close Date/Time	Pips W/L	Profit/ Loss	New Balance

TRADE SETUP NOTES:

ADDITIONAL NOTES:

TRADING LOG

Order Date/Time	Pair	Order Ticket #	Buy/ Sell	Lots/ Units	Entry Price	Exit Price	Close Date/Time	Pips W/L	Profit/ Loss	New Balance

TRADE SETUP NOTES:

ADDITIONAL NOTES:

Order Date/Time	Pair	Order Ticket #	Buy/ Sell	Lots/ Units	Entry Price	Exit Price	Close Date/Time	Pips W/L	Profit/ Loss	New Balance

TRADE SETUP NOTES:

ADDITIONAL NOTES:

Order Date/Time	Pair	Order Ticket #	Buy/ Sell	Lots/ Units	Entry Price	Exit Price	Close Date/Time	Pips W/L	Profit/ Loss	New Balance

TRADE SETUP NOTES:

ADDITIONAL NOTES:

Order Date/Time	Pair	Order Ticket #	Buy/ Sell	Lots/ Units	Entry Price	Exit Price	Close Date/Time	Pips W/L	Profit/ Loss	New Balance

TRADE SETUP NOTES:

ADDITIONAL NOTES:

Order Date/Time	Pair	Order Ticket #	Buy/ Sell	Lots/ Units	Entry Price	Exit Price	Close Date/Time	Pips W/L	Profit/ Loss	New Balance

TRADE SETUP NOTES:

ADDITIONAL NOTES:

Order Date/Time	Pair	Order Ticket #	Buy/ Sell	Lots/ Units	Entry Price	Exit Price	Close Date/Time	Pips W/L	Profit/ Loss	New Balance

TRADE SETUP NOTES:

ADDITIONAL NOTES:

TRADING LOG

Order Date/Time	Pair	Order Ticket #	Buy/ Sell	Lots/ Units	Entry Price	Exit Price	Close Date/Time	Pips W/L	Profit/ Loss	New Balance

TRADE SETUP NOTES:

ADDITIONAL NOTES:

Order Date/Time	Pair	Order Ticket #	Buy/ Sell	Lots/ Units	Entry Price	Exit Price	Close Date/Time	Pips W/L	Profit/ Loss	New Balance

TRADE SETUP NOTES:

ADDITIONAL NOTES:

Order Date/Time	Pair	Order Ticket #	Buy/ Sell	Lots/ Units	Entry Price	Exit Price	Close Date/Time	Pips W/L	Profit/ Loss	New Balance

TRADE SETUP NOTES:

ADDITIONAL NOTES:

Order Date/Time	Pair	Order Ticket #	Buy/ Sell	Lots/ Units	Entry Price	Exit Price	Close Date/Time	Pips W/L	Profit/ Loss	New Balance

TRADE SETUP NOTES:

ADDITIONAL NOTES:

Order Date/Time	Pair	Order Ticket #	Buy/ Sell	Lots/ Units	Entry Price	Exit Price	Close Date/Time	Pips W/L	Profit/ Loss	New Balance

TRADE SETUP NOTES:

ADDITIONAL NOTES:

Order Date/Time	Pair	Order Ticket #	Buy/ Sell	Lots/ Units	Entry Price	Exit Price	Close Date/Time	Pips W/L	Profit/ Loss	New Balance

TRADE SETUP NOTES:

ADDITIONAL NOTES:

TRADING LOG

Order Date/Time	Pair	Order Ticket #	Buy/ Sell	Lots/ Units	Entry Price	Exit Price	Close Date/Time	Pips W/L	Profit/ Loss	New Balance

TRADE SETUP NOTES:

ADDITIONAL NOTES:

Order Date/Time	Pair	Order Ticket #	Buy/ Sell	Lots/ Units	Entry Price	Exit Price	Close Date/Time	Pips W/L	Profit/ Loss	New Balance

TRADE SETUP NOTES:

ADDITIONAL NOTES:

Order Date/Time	Pair	Order Ticket #	Buy/ Sell	Lots/ Units	Entry Price	Exit Price	Close Date/Time	Pips W/L	Profit/ Loss	New Balance

TRADE SETUP NOTES:

ADDITIONAL NOTES:

Order Date/Time	Pair	Order Ticket #	Buy/ Sell	Lots/ Units	Entry Price	Exit Price	Close Date/Time	Pips W/L	Profit/ Loss	New Balance

TRADE SETUP NOTES:

ADDITIONAL NOTES:

Order Date/Time	Pair	Order Ticket #	Buy/ Sell	Lots/ Units	Entry Price	Exit Price	Close Date/Time	Pips W/L	Profit/ Loss	New Balance

TRADE SETUP NOTES:

ADDITIONAL NOTES:

Order Date/Time	Pair	Order Ticket #	Buy/ Sell	Lots/ Units	Entry Price	Exit Price	Close Date/Time	Pips W/L	Profit/ Loss	New Balance

TRADE SETUP NOTES:

ADDITIONAL NOTES:

Order Date/Time	Pair	Order Ticket #	Buy/ Sell	Lots/ Units	Entry Price	Exit Price	Close Date/Time	Pips W/L	Profit/ Loss	New Balance

TRADE SETUP NOTES:

ADDITIONAL NOTES:

TRADING LOG

Order Date/Time	Pair	Order Ticket #	Buy/ Sell	Lots/ Units	Entry Price	Exit Price	Close Date/Time	Pips W/L	Profit/ Loss	New Balance

TRADE SETUP NOTES:

ADDITIONAL NOTES:

Order Date/Time	Pair	Order Ticket #	Buy/ Sell	Lots/ Units	Entry Price	Exit Price	Close Date/Time	Pips W/L	Profit/ Loss	New Balance

TRADE SETUP NOTES:

ADDITIONAL NOTES:

Order Date/Time	Pair	Order Ticket #	Buy/ Sell	Lots/ Units	Entry Price	Exit Price	Close Date/Time	Pips W/L	Profit/ Loss	New Balance

TRADE SETUP NOTES:

ADDITIONAL NOTES:

Order Date/Time	Pair	Order Ticket #	Buy/ Sell	Lots/ Units	Entry Price	Exit Price	Close Date/Time	Pips W/L	Profit/ Loss	New Balance

TRADE SETUP NOTES:

ADDITIONAL NOTES:

Order Date/Time	Pair	Order Ticket #	Buy/ Sell	Lots/ Units	Entry Price	Exit Price	Close Date/Time	Pips W/L	Profit/ Loss	New Balance

TRADE SETUP NOTES:

ADDITIONAL NOTES:

Order Date/Time	Pair	Order Ticket #	Buy/ Sell	Lots/ Units	Entry Price	Exit Price	Close Date/Time	Pips W/L	Profit/ Loss	New Balance

TRADE SETUP NOTES:

ADDITIONAL NOTES:

Order Date/Time	Pair	Order Ticket #	Buy/ Sell	Lots/ Units	Entry Price	Exit Price	Close Date/Time	Pips W/L	Profit/ Loss	New Balance

TRADE SETUP NOTES:

ADDITIONAL NOTES:

TRADING LOG

Order Date/Time	Pair	Order Ticket #	Buy/ Sell	Lots/ Units	Entry Price	Exit Price	Close Date/Time	Pips W/L	Profit/ Loss	New Balance

TRADE SETUP NOTES:

ADDITIONAL NOTES:

Order Date/Time	Pair	Order Ticket #	Buy/ Sell	Lots/ Units	Entry Price	Exit Price	Close Date/Time	Pips W/L	Profit/ Loss	New Balance

TRADE SETUP NOTES:

ADDITIONAL NOTES:

Order Date/Time	Pair	Order Ticket #	Buy/ Sell	Lots/ Units	Entry Price	Exit Price	Close Date/Time	Pips W/L	Profit/ Loss	New Balance

TRADE SETUP NOTES:

ADDITIONAL NOTES:

Order Date/Time	Pair	Order Ticket #	Buy/ Sell	Lots/ Units	Entry Price	Exit Price	Close Date/Time	Pips W/L	Profit/ Loss	New Balance

TRADE SETUP NOTES:

ADDITIONAL NOTES:

Order Date/Time	Pair	Order Ticket #	Buy/ Sell	Lots/ Units	Entry Price	Exit Price	Close Date/Time	Pips W/L	Profit/ Loss	New Balance

TRADE SETUP NOTES:

ADDITIONAL NOTES:

Order Date/Time	Pair	Order Ticket #	Buy/ Sell	Lots/ Units	Entry Price	Exit Price	Close Date/Time	Pips W/L	Profit/ Loss	New Balance

TRADE SETUP NOTES:

ADDITIONAL NOTES:

Order Date/Time	Pair	Order Ticket #	Buy/ Sell	Lots/ Units	Entry Price	Exit Price	Close Date/Time	Pips W/L	Profit/ Loss	New Balance

TRADE SETUP NOTES:

ADDITIONAL NOTES:

TRADING LOG

Order Date/Time	Pair	Order Ticket #	Buy/ Sell	Lots/ Units	Entry Price	Exit Price	Close Date/Time	Pips W/L	Profit/ Loss	New Balance

TRADE SETUP NOTES:

ADDITIONAL NOTES:

Order Date/Time	Pair	Order Ticket #	Buy/ Sell	Lots/ Units	Entry Price	Exit Price	Close Date/Time	Pips W/L	Profit/ Loss	New Balance

TRADE SETUP NOTES:

ADDITIONAL NOTES:

Order Date/Time	Pair	Order Ticket #	Buy/ Sell	Lots/ Units	Entry Price	Exit Price	Close Date/Time	Pips W/L	Profit/ Loss	New Balance

TRADE SETUP NOTES:

ADDITIONAL NOTES:

Order Date/Time	Pair	Order Ticket #	Buy/ Sell	Lots/ Units	Entry Price	Exit Price	Close Date/Time	Pips W/L	Profit/ Loss	New Balance

TRADE SETUP NOTES:

ADDITIONAL NOTES:

Order Date/Time	Pair	Order Ticket #	Buy/ Sell	Lots/ Units	Entry Price	Exit Price	Close Date/Time	Pips W/L	Profit/ Loss	New Balance

TRADE SETUP NOTES:

ADDITIONAL NOTES:

Order Date/Time	Pair	Order Ticket #	Buy/ Sell	Lots/ Units	Entry Price	Exit Price	Close Date/Time	Pips W/L	Profit/ Loss	New Balance

TRADE SETUP NOTES:

ADDITIONAL NOTES:

TRADING LOG

Order Date/Time	Pair	Order Ticket #	Buy/ Sell	Lots/ Units	Entry Price	Exit Price	Close Date/Time	Pips W/L	Profit/ Loss	New Balance

TRADE SETUP NOTES:

ADDITIONAL NOTES:

Order Date/Time	Pair	Order Ticket #	Buy/ Sell	Lots/ Units	Entry Price	Exit Price	Close Date/Time	Pips W/L	Profit/ Loss	New Balance

TRADE SETUP NOTES:

ADDITIONAL NOTES:

Order Date/Time	Pair	Order Ticket #	Buy/ Sell	Lots/ Units	Entry Price	Exit Price	Close Date/Time	Pips W/L	Profit/ Loss	New Balance

TRADE SETUP NOTES:

ADDITIONAL NOTES:

Order Date/Time	Pair	Order Ticket #	Buy/ Sell	Lots/ Units	Entry Price	Exit Price	Close Date/Time	Pips W/L	Profit/ Loss	New Balance

TRADE SETUP NOTES:

ADDITIONAL NOTES:

Order Date/Time	Pair	Order Ticket #	Buy/ Sell	Lots/ Units	Entry Price	Exit Price	Close Date/Time	Pips W/L	Profit/ Loss	New Balance

TRADE SETUP NOTES:

ADDITIONAL NOTES:

Order Date/Time	Pair	Order Ticket #	Buy/ Sell	Lots/ Units	Entry Price	Exit Price	Close Date/Time	Pips W/L	Profit/ Loss	New Balance

TRADE SETUP NOTES:

ADDITIONAL NOTES:

TRADING LOG

Order Date/Time	Pair	Order Ticket #	Buy/ Sell	Lots/ Units	Entry Price	Exit Price	Close Date/Time	Pips W/L	Profit/ Loss	New Balance

TRADE SETUP NOTES:

ADDITIONAL NOTES:

Order Date/Time	Pair	Order Ticket #	Buy/ Sell	Lots/ Units	Entry Price	Exit Price	Close Date/Time	Pips W/L	Profit/ Loss	New Balance

TRADE SETUP NOTES:

ADDITIONAL NOTES:

Order Date/Time	Pair	Order Ticket #	Buy/ Sell	Lots/ Units	Entry Price	Exit Price	Close Date/Time	Pips W/L	Profit/ Loss	New Balance

TRADE SETUP NOTES:

ADDITIONAL NOTES:

Order Date/Time	Pair	Order Ticket #	Buy/ Sell	Lots/ Units	Entry Price	Exit Price	Close Date/Time	Pips W/L	Profit/ Loss	New Balance

TRADE SETUP NOTES:

ADDITIONAL NOTES:

Order Date/Time	Pair	Order Ticket #	Buy/ Sell	Lots/ Units	Entry Price	Exit Price	Close Date/Time	Pips W/L	Profit/ Loss	New Balance

TRADE SETUP NOTES:

ADDITIONAL NOTES:

Order Date/Time	Pair	Order Ticket #	Buy/ Sell	Lots/ Units	Entry Price	Exit Price	Close Date/Time	Pips W/L	Profit/ Loss	New Balance

TRADE SETUP NOTES:

ADDITIONAL NOTES:

TRADING LOG

Order Date/Time	Pair	Order Ticket #	Buy/ Sell	Lots/ Units	Entry Price	Exit Price	Close Date/Time	Pips W/L	Profit/ Loss	New Balance

TRADE SETUP NOTES:

ADDITIONAL NOTES:

Order Date/Time	Pair	Order Ticket #	Buy/ Sell	Lots/ Units	Entry Price	Exit Price	Close Date/Time	Pips W/L	Profit/ Loss	New Balance

TRADE SETUP NOTES:

ADDITIONAL NOTES:

Order Date/Time	Pair	Order Ticket #	Buy/ Sell	Lots/ Units	Entry Price	Exit Price	Close Date/Time	Pips W/L	Profit/ Loss	New Balance

TRADE SETUP NOTES:

ADDITIONAL NOTES:

Order Date/Time	Pair	Order Ticket #	Buy/ Sell	Lots/ Units	Entry Price	Exit Price	Close Date/Time	Pips W/L	Profit/ Loss	New Balance

TRADE SETUP NOTES:

ADDITIONAL NOTES:

Order Date/Time	Pair	Order Ticket #	Buy/ Sell	Lots/ Units	Entry Price	Exit Price	Close Date/Time	Pips W/L	Profit/ Loss	New Balance

TRADE SETUP NOTES:

ADDITIONAL NOTES:

Order Date/Time	Pair	Order Ticket #	Buy/ Sell	Lots/ Units	Entry Price	Exit Price	Close Date/Time	Pips W/L	Profit/ Loss	New Balance

TRADE SETUP NOTES:

ADDITIONAL NOTES:

Order Date/Time	Pair	Order Ticket #	Buy/ Sell	Lots/ Units	Entry Price	Exit Price	Close Date/Time	Pips W/L	Profit/ Loss	New Balance

TRADE SETUP NOTES:

ADDITIONAL NOTES:

TRADING LOG

Order Date/Time	Pair	Order Ticket #	Buy/ Sell	Lots/ Units	Entry Price	Exit Price	Close Date/Time	Pips W/L	Profit/ Loss	New Balance

TRADE SETUP NOTES:

ADDITIONAL NOTES:

Order Date/Time	Pair	Order Ticket #	Buy/ Sell	Lots/ Units	Entry Price	Exit Price	Close Date/Time	Pips W/L	Profit/ Loss	New Balance

TRADE SETUP NOTES:

ADDITIONAL NOTES:

Order Date/Time	Pair	Order Ticket #	Buy/ Sell	Lots/ Units	Entry Price	Exit Price	Close Date/Time	Pips W/L	Profit/ Loss	New Balance

TRADE SETUP NOTES:

ADDITIONAL NOTES:

Order Date/Time	Pair	Order Ticket #	Buy/ Sell	Lots/ Units	Entry Price	Exit Price	Close Date/Time	Pips W/L	Profit/ Loss	New Balance

TRADE SETUP NOTES:

ADDITIONAL NOTES:

Order Date/Time	Pair	Order Ticket #	Buy/ Sell	Lots/ Units	Entry Price	Exit Price	Close Date/Time	Pips W/L	Profit/ Loss	New Balance

TRADE SETUP NOTES:

ADDITIONAL NOTES:

Order Date/Time	Pair	Order Ticket #	Buy/ Sell	Lots/ Units	Entry Price	Exit Price	Close Date/Time	Pips W/L	Profit/ Loss	New Balance

TRADE SETUP NOTES:

ADDITIONAL NOTES:

TRADING LOG

Order Date/Time	Pair	Order Ticket #	Buy/ Sell	Lots/ Units	Entry Price	Exit Price	Close Date/Time	Pips W/L	Profit/ Loss	New Balance

TRADE SETUP NOTES:

ADDITIONAL NOTES:

Order Date/Time	Pair	Order Ticket #	Buy/ Sell	Lots/ Units	Entry Price	Exit Price	Close Date/Time	Pips W/L	Profit/ Loss	New Balance

TRADE SETUP NOTES:

ADDITIONAL NOTES:

Order Date/Time	Pair	Order Ticket #	Buy/ Sell	Lots/ Units	Entry Price	Exit Price	Close Date/Time	Pips W/L	Profit/ Loss	New Balance

TRADE SETUP NOTES:

ADDITIONAL NOTES:

Order Date/Time	Pair	Order Ticket #	Buy/ Sell	Lots/ Units	Entry Price	Exit Price	Close Date/Time	Pips W/L	Profit/ Loss	New Balance

TRADE SETUP NOTES:

ADDITIONAL NOTES:

Order Date/Time	Pair	Order Ticket #	Buy/ Sell	Lots/ Units	Entry Price	Exit Price	Close Date/Time	Pips W/L	Profit/ Loss	New Balance

TRADE SETUP NOTES:

ADDITIONAL NOTES:

Order Date/Time	Pair	Order Ticket #	Buy/ Sell	Lots/ Units	Entry Price	Exit Price	Close Date/Time	Pips W/L	Profit/ Loss	New Balance

TRADE SETUP NOTES:

ADDITIONAL NOTES:

TRADING LOG

Order Date/Time	Pair	Order Ticket #	Buy/ Sell	Lots/ Units	Entry Price	Exit Price	Close Date/Time	Pips W/L	Profit/ Loss	New Balance

TRADE SETUP NOTES:

ADDITIONAL NOTES:

Order Date/Time	Pair	Order Ticket #	Buy/ Sell	Lots/ Units	Entry Price	Exit Price	Close Date/Time	Pips W/L	Profit/ Loss	New Balance

TRADE SETUP NOTES:

ADDITIONAL NOTES:

Order Date/Time	Pair	Order Ticket #	Buy/ Sell	Lots/ Units	Entry Price	Exit Price	Close Date/Time	Pips W/L	Profit/ Loss	New Balance

TRADE SETUP NOTES:

ADDITIONAL NOTES:

Order Date/Time	Pair	Order Ticket #	Buy/ Sell	Lots/ Units	Entry Price	Exit Price	Close Date/Time	Pips W/L	Profit/ Loss	New Balance

TRADE SETUP NOTES:

ADDITIONAL NOTES:

Order Date/Time	Pair	Order Ticket #	Buy/ Sell	Lots/ Units	Entry Price	Exit Price	Close Date/Time	Pips W/L	Profit/ Loss	New Balance

TRADE SETUP NOTES:

ADDITIONAL NOTES:

Order Date/Time	Pair	Order Ticket #	Buy/ Sell	Lots/ Units	Entry Price	Exit Price	Close Date/Time	Pips W/L	Profit/ Loss	New Balance

TRADE SETUP NOTES:

ADDITIONAL NOTES:

TRADING LOG

Order Date/Time	Pair	Order Ticket #	Buy/ Sell	Lots/ Units	Entry Price	Exit Price	Close Date/Time	Pips W/L	Profit/ Loss	New Balance

TRADE SETUP NOTES:

ADDITIONAl NOTES:

Order Date/Time	Pair	Order Ticket #	Buy/ Sell	Lots/ Units	Entry Price	Exit Price	Close Date/Time	Pips W/L	Profit/ Loss	New Balance

TRADE SETUP NOTES:

ADDITIONAl NOTES:

Order Date/Time	Pair	Order Ticket #	Buy/ Sell	Lots/ Units	Entry Price	Exit Price	Close Date/Time	Pips W/L	Profit/ Loss	New Balance

TRADE SETUP NOTES:

ADDITIONAl NOTES:

Order Date/Time	Pair	Order Ticket #	Buy/ Sell	Lots/ Units	Entry Price	Exit Price	Close Date/Time	Pips W/L	Profit/ Loss	New Balance

TRADE SETUP NOTES:

ADDITIONAl NOTES:

Order Date/Time	Pair	Order Ticket #	Buy/ Sell	Lots/ Units	Entry Price	Exit Price	Close Date/Time	Pips W/L	Profit/ Loss	New Balance

TRADE SETUP NOTES:

ADDITIONAl NOTES:

Order Date/Time	Pair	Order Ticket #	Buy/ Sell	Lots/ Units	Entry Price	Exit Price	Close Date/Time	Pips W/L	Profit/ Loss	New Balance

TRADE SETUP NOTES:

ADDITIONAl NOTES:

Order Date/Time	Pair	Order Ticket #	Buy/ Sell	Lots/ Units	Entry Price	Exit Price	Close Date/Time	Pips W/L	Profit/ Loss	New Balance

TRADE SETUP NOTES:

ADDITIONAl NOTES:

TRADING LOG

Order Date/Time	Pair	Order Ticket #	Buy/ Sell	Lots/ Units	Entry Price	Exit Price	Close Date/Time	Pips W/L	Profit/ Loss	New Balance

TRADE SETUP NOTES:

ADDITIONAL NOTES:

Order Date/Time	Pair	Order Ticket #	Buy/ Sell	Lots/ Units	Entry Price	Exit Price	Close Date/Time	Pips W/L	Profit/ Loss	New Balance

TRADE SETUP NOTES:

ADDITIONAL NOTES:

Order Date/Time	Pair	Order Ticket #	Buy/ Sell	Lots/ Units	Entry Price	Exit Price	Close Date/Time	Pips W/L	Profit/ Loss	New Balance

TRADE SETUP NOTES:

ADDITIONAL NOTES:

Order Date/Time	Pair	Order Ticket #	Buy/ Sell	Lots/ Units	Entry Price	Exit Price	Close Date/Time	Pips W/L	Profit/ Loss	New Balance

TRADE SETUP NOTES:

ADDITIONAL NOTES:

Order Date/Time	Pair	Order Ticket #	Buy/ Sell	Lots/ Units	Entry Price	Exit Price	Close Date/Time	Pips W/L	Profit/ Loss	New Balance

TRADE SETUP NOTES:

ADDITIONAL NOTES:

Order Date/Time	Pair	Order Ticket #	Buy/ Sell	Lots/ Units	Entry Price	Exit Price	Close Date/Time	Pips W/L	Profit/ Loss	New Balance

TRADE SETUP NOTES:

ADDITIONAL NOTES:

TRADING LOG

Order Date/Time	Pair	Order Ticket #	Buy/ Sell	Lots/ Units	Entry Price	Exit Price	Close Date/Time	Pips W/L	Profit/ Loss	New Balance

TRADE SETUP NOTES:

ADDITIONAL NOTES:

Order Date/Time	Pair	Order Ticket #	Buy/ Sell	Lots/ Units	Entry Price	Exit Price	Close Date/Time	Pips W/L	Profit/ Loss	New Balance

TRADE SETUP NOTES:

ADDITIONAL NOTES:

Order Date/Time	Pair	Order Ticket #	Buy/ Sell	Lots/ Units	Entry Price	Exit Price	Close Date/Time	Pips W/L	Profit/ Loss	New Balance

TRADE SETUP NOTES:

ADDITIONAL NOTES:

Order Date/Time	Pair	Order Ticket #	Buy/ Sell	Lots/ Units	Entry Price	Exit Price	Close Date/Time	Pips W/L	Profit/ Loss	New Balance

TRADE SETUP NOTES:

ADDITIONAL NOTES:

Order Date/Time	Pair	Order Ticket #	Buy/ Sell	Lots/ Units	Entry Price	Exit Price	Close Date/Time	Pips W/L	Profit/ Loss	New Balance

TRADE SETUP NOTES:

ADDITIONAL NOTES:

Order Date/Time	Pair	Order Ticket #	Buy/ Sell	Lots/ Units	Entry Price	Exit Price	Close Date/Time	Pips W/L	Profit/ Loss	New Balance

TRADE SETUP NOTES:

ADDITIONAL NOTES:

TRADING LOG

Order Date/Time	Pair	Order Ticket #	Buy/ Sell	Lots/ Units	Entry Price	Exit Price	Close Date/Time	Pips W/L	Profit/ Loss	New Balance

TRADE SETUP NOTES:

ADDITIONAL NOTES:

Order Date/Time	Pair	Order Ticket #	Buy/ Sell	Lots/ Units	Entry Price	Exit Price	Close Date/Time	Pips W/L	Profit/ Loss	New Balance

TRADE SETUP NOTES:

ADDITIONAL NOTES:

Order Date/Time	Pair	Order Ticket #	Buy/ Sell	Lots/ Units	Entry Price	Exit Price	Close Date/Time	Pips W/L	Profit/ Loss	New Balance

TRADE SETUP NOTES:

ADDITIONAL NOTES:

Order Date/Time	Pair	Order Ticket #	Buy/ Sell	Lots/ Units	Entry Price	Exit Price	Close Date/Time	Pips W/L	Profit/ Loss	New Balance

TRADE SETUP NOTES:

ADDITIONAL NOTES:

Order Date/Time	Pair	Order Ticket #	Buy/ Sell	Lots/ Units	Entry Price	Exit Price	Close Date/Time	Pips W/L	Profit/ Loss	New Balance

TRADE SETUP NOTES:

ADDITIONAL NOTES:

Order Date/Time	Pair	Order Ticket #	Buy/ Sell	Lots/ Units	Entry Price	Exit Price	Close Date/Time	Pips W/L	Profit/ Loss	New Balance

TRADE SETUP NOTES:

ADDITIONAL NOTES:

TRADING LOG

Order Date/Time	Pair	Order Ticket #	Buy/ Sell	Lots/ Units	Entry Price	Exit Price	Close Date/Time	Pips W/L	Profit/ Loss	New Balance

TRADE SETUP NOTES:

ADDITIONAL NOTES:

Order Date/Time	Pair	Order Ticket #	Buy/ Sell	Lots/ Units	Entry Price	Exit Price	Close Date/Time	Pips W/L	Profit/ Loss	New Balance

TRADE SETUP NOTES:

ADDITIONAL NOTES:

Order Date/Time	Pair	Order Ticket #	Buy/ Sell	Lots/ Units	Entry Price	Exit Price	Close Date/Time	Pips W/L	Profit/ Loss	New Balance

TRADE SETUP NOTES:

ADDITIONAL NOTES:

Order Date/Time	Pair	Order Ticket #	Buy/ Sell	Lots/ Units	Entry Price	Exit Price	Close Date/Time	Pips W/L	Profit/ Loss	New Balance

TRADE SETUP NOTES:

ADDITIONAL NOTES:

Order Date/Time	Pair	Order Ticket #	Buy/ Sell	Lots/ Units	Entry Price	Exit Price	Close Date/Time	Pips W/L	Profit/ Loss	New Balance

TRADE SETUP NOTES:

ADDITIONAL NOTES:

Order Date/Time	Pair	Order Ticket #	Buy/ Sell	Lots/ Units	Entry Price	Exit Price	Close Date/Time	Pips W/L	Profit/ Loss	New Balance

TRADE SETUP NOTES:

ADDITIONAL NOTES:

TRADING LOG

Order Date/Time	Pair	Order Ticket #	Buy/ Sell	Lots/ Units	Entry Price	Exit Price	Close Date/Time	Pips W/L	Profit/ Loss	New Balance

TRADE SETUP NOTES:

ADDITIONAL NOTES:

Order Date/Time	Pair	Order Ticket #	Buy/ Sell	Lots/ Units	Entry Price	Exit Price	Close Date/Time	Pips W/L	Profit/ Loss	New Balance

TRADE SETUP NOTES:

ADDITIONAL NOTES:

Order Date/Time	Pair	Order Ticket #	Buy/ Sell	Lots/ Units	Entry Price	Exit Price	Close Date/Time	Pips W/L	Profit/ Loss	New Balance

TRADE SETUP NOTES:

ADDITIONAL NOTES:

Order Date/Time	Pair	Order Ticket #	Buy/ Sell	Lots/ Units	Entry Price	Exit Price	Close Date/Time	Pips W/L	Profit/ Loss	New Balance

TRADE SETUP NOTES:

ADDITIONAL NOTES:

Order Date/Time	Pair	Order Ticket #	Buy/ Sell	Lots/ Units	Entry Price	Exit Price	Close Date/Time	Pips W/L	Profit/ Loss	New Balance

TRADE SETUP NOTES:

ADDITIONAL NOTES:

Order Date/Time	Pair	Order Ticket #	Buy/ Sell	Lots/ Units	Entry Price	Exit Price	Close Date/Time	Pips W/L	Profit/ Loss	New Balance

TRADE SETUP NOTES:

ADDITIONAL NOTES:

TRADING LOG

Order Date/Time	Pair	Order Ticket #	Buy/ Sell	Lots/ Units	Entry Price	Exit Price	Close Date/Time	Pips W/L	Profit/ Loss	New Balance

TRADE SETUP NOTES:

ADDITIONAL NOTES:

Order Date/Time	Pair	Order Ticket #	Buy/ Sell	Lots/ Units	Entry Price	Exit Price	Close Date/Time	Pips W/L	Profit/ Loss	New Balance

TRADE SETUP NOTES:

ADDITIONAL NOTES:

Order Date/Time	Pair	Order Ticket #	Buy/ Sell	Lots/ Units	Entry Price	Exit Price	Close Date/Time	Pips W/L	Profit/ Loss	New Balance

TRADE SETUP NOTES:

ADDITIONAL NOTES:

Order Date/Time	Pair	Order Ticket #	Buy/ Sell	Lots/ Units	Entry Price	Exit Price	Close Date/Time	Pips W/L	Profit/ Loss	New Balance

TRADE SETUP NOTES:

ADDITIONAL NOTES:

Order Date/Time	Pair	Order Ticket #	Buy/ Sell	Lots/ Units	Entry Price	Exit Price	Close Date/Time	Pips W/L	Profit/ Loss	New Balance

TRADE SETUP NOTES:

ADDITIONAL NOTES:

Order Date/Time	Pair	Order Ticket #	Buy/ Sell	Lots/ Units	Entry Price	Exit Price	Close Date/Time	Pips W/L	Profit/ Loss	New Balance

TRADE SETUP NOTES:

ADDITIONAL NOTES:

Order Date/Time	Pair	Order Ticket #	Buy/ Sell	Lots/ Units	Entry Price	Exit Price	Close Date/Time	Pips W/L	Profit/ Loss	New Balance

TRADE SETUP NOTES:

ADDITIONAL NOTES:

TRADING LOG

Order Date/Time	Pair	Order Ticket #	Buy/ Sell	Lots/ Units	Entry Price	Exit Price	Close Date/Time	Pips W/L	Profit/ Loss	New Balance

TRADE SETUP NOTES:

ADDITIONAL NOTES:

Order Date/Time	Pair	Order Ticket #	Buy/ Sell	Lots/ Units	Entry Price	Exit Price	Close Date/Time	Pips W/L	Profit/ Loss	New Balance

TRADE SETUP NOTES:

ADDITIONAL NOTES:

Order Date/Time	Pair	Order Ticket #	Buy/ Sell	Lots/ Units	Entry Price	Exit Price	Close Date/Time	Pips W/L	Profit/ Loss	New Balance

TRADE SETUP NOTES:

ADDITIONAL NOTES:

Order Date/Time	Pair	Order Ticket #	Buy/ Sell	Lots/ Units	Entry Price	Exit Price	Close Date/Time	Pips W/L	Profit/ Loss	New Balance

TRADE SETUP NOTES:

ADDITIONAL NOTES:

Order Date/Time	Pair	Order Ticket #	Buy/ Sell	Lots/ Units	Entry Price	Exit Price	Close Date/Time	Pips W/L	Profit/ Loss	New Balance

TRADE SETUP NOTES:

ADDITIONAL NOTES:

Order Date/Time	Pair	Order Ticket #	Buy/ Sell	Lots/ Units	Entry Price	Exit Price	Close Date/Time	Pips W/L	Profit/ Loss	New Balance

TRADE SETUP NOTES:

ADDITIONAL NOTES:

TRADING LOG

Order Date/Time	Pair	Order Ticket #	Buy/ Sell	Lots/ Units	Entry Price	Exit Price	Close Date/Time	Pips W/L	Profit/ Loss	New Balance

TRADE SETUP NOTES:

ADDITIONAL NOTES:

Order Date/Time	Pair	Order Ticket #	Buy/ Sell	Lots/ Units	Entry Price	Exit Price	Close Date/Time	Pips W/L	Profit/ Loss	New Balance

TRADE SETUP NOTES:

ADDITIONAL NOTES:

Order Date/Time	Pair	Order Ticket #	Buy/ Sell	Lots/ Units	Entry Price	Exit Price	Close Date/Time	Pips W/L	Profit/ Loss	New Balance

TRADE SETUP NOTES:

ADDITIONAL NOTES:

Order Date/Time	Pair	Order Ticket #	Buy/ Sell	Lots/ Units	Entry Price	Exit Price	Close Date/Time	Pips W/L	Profit/ Loss	New Balance

TRADE SETUP NOTES:

ADDITIONAL NOTES:

Order Date/Time	Pair	Order Ticket #	Buy/ Sell	Lots/ Units	Entry Price	Exit Price	Close Date/Time	Pips W/L	Profit/ Loss	New Balance

TRADE SETUP NOTES:

ADDITIONAL NOTES:

Order Date/Time	Pair	Order Ticket #	Buy/ Sell	Lots/ Units	Entry Price	Exit Price	Close Date/Time	Pips W/L	Profit/ Loss	New Balance

TRADE SETUP NOTES:

ADDITIONAL NOTES:

TRADING LOG

Order Date/Time	Pair	Order Ticket #	Buy/ Sell	Lots/ Units	Entry Price	Exit Price	Close Date/Time	Pips W/L	Profit/ Loss	New Balance

TRADE SETUP NOTES:

ADDITIONAL NOTES:

Order Date/Time	Pair	Order Ticket #	Buy/ Sell	Lots/ Units	Entry Price	Exit Price	Close Date/Time	Pips W/L	Profit/ Loss	New Balance

TRADE SETUP NOTES:

ADDITIONAL NOTES:

Order Date/Time	Pair	Order Ticket #	Buy/ Sell	Lots/ Units	Entry Price	Exit Price	Close Date/Time	Pips W/L	Profit/ Loss	New Balance

TRADE SETUP NOTES:

ADDITIONAL NOTES:

Order Date/Time	Pair	Order Ticket #	Buy/ Sell	Lots/ Units	Entry Price	Exit Price	Close Date/Time	Pips W/L	Profit/ Loss	New Balance

TRADE SETUP NOTES:

ADDITIONAL NOTES:

Order Date/Time	Pair	Order Ticket #	Buy/ Sell	Lots/ Units	Entry Price	Exit Price	Close Date/Time	Pips W/L	Profit/ Loss	New Balance

TRADE SETUP NOTES:

ADDITIONAL NOTES:

Order Date/Time	Pair	Order Ticket #	Buy/ Sell	Lots/ Units	Entry Price	Exit Price	Close Date/Time	Pips W/L	Profit/ Loss	New Balance

TRADE SETUP NOTES:

ADDITIONAL NOTES:

TRADING LOG

Order Date/Time	Pair	Order Ticket #	Buy/ Sell	Lots/ Units	Entry Price	Exit Price	Close Date/Time	Pips W/L	Profit/ Loss	New Balance

TRADE SETUP NOTES:

ADDITIONAL NOTES:

Order Date/Time	Pair	Order Ticket #	Buy/ Sell	Lots/ Units	Entry Price	Exit Price	Close Date/Time	Pips W/L	Profit/ Loss	New Balance

TRADE SETUP NOTES:

ADDITIONAL NOTES:

Order Date/Time	Pair	Order Ticket #	Buy/ Sell	Lots/ Units	Entry Price	Exit Price	Close Date/Time	Pips W/L	Profit/ Loss	New Balance

TRADE SETUP NOTES:

ADDITIONAL NOTES:

Order Date/Time	Pair	Order Ticket #	Buy/ Sell	Lots/ Units	Entry Price	Exit Price	Close Date/Time	Pips W/L	Profit/ Loss	New Balance

TRADE SETUP NOTES:

ADDITIONAL NOTES:

Order Date/Time	Pair	Order Ticket #	Buy/ Sell	Lots/ Units	Entry Price	Exit Price	Close Date/Time	Pips W/L	Profit/ Loss	New Balance

TRADE SETUP NOTES:

ADDITIONAL NOTES:

Order Date/Time	Pair	Order Ticket #	Buy/ Sell	Lots/ Units	Entry Price	Exit Price	Close Date/Time	Pips W/L	Profit/ Loss	New Balance

TRADE SETUP NOTES:

ADDITIONAL NOTES:

Order Date/Time	Pair	Order Ticket #	Buy/ Sell	Lots/ Units	Entry Price	Exit Price	Close Date/Time	Pips W/L	Profit/ Loss	New Balance

TRADE SETUP NOTES:

ADDITIONAL NOTES:

TRADING LOG

Order Date/Time	Pair	Order Ticket #	Buy/Sell	Lots/Units	Entry Price	Exit Price	Close Date/Time	Pips W/L	Profit/Loss	New Balance

TRADE SETUP NOTES:

ADDITIONAL NOTES:

Order Date/Time	Pair	Order Ticket #	Buy/Sell	Lots/Units	Entry Price	Exit Price	Close Date/Time	Pips W/L	Profit/Loss	New Balance

TRADE SETUP NOTES:

ADDITIONAL NOTES:

Order Date/Time	Pair	Order Ticket #	Buy/Sell	Lots/Units	Entry Price	Exit Price	Close Date/Time	Pips W/L	Profit/Loss	New Balance

TRADE SETUP NOTES:

ADDITIONAL NOTES:

Order Date/Time	Pair	Order Ticket #	Buy/Sell	Lots/Units	Entry Price	Exit Price	Close Date/Time	Pips W/L	Profit/Loss	New Balance

TRADE SETUP NOTES:

ADDITIONAL NOTES:

Order Date/Time	Pair	Order Ticket #	Buy/Sell	Lots/Units	Entry Price	Exit Price	Close Date/Time	Pips W/L	Profit/Loss	New Balance

TRADE SETUP NOTES:

ADDITIONAL NOTES:

Order Date/Time	Pair	Order Ticket #	Buy/Sell	Lots/Units	Entry Price	Exit Price	Close Date/Time	Pips W/L	Profit/Loss	New Balance

TRADE SETUP NOTES:

ADDITIONAL NOTES:

TRADING LOG

Order Date/Time	Pair	Order Ticket #	Buy/ Sell	Lots/ Units	Entry Price	Exit Price	Close Date/Time	Pips W/L	Profit/ Loss	New Balance

TRADE SETUP NOTES:

ADDITIONAL NOTES:

Order Date/Time	Pair	Order Ticket #	Buy/ Sell	Lots/ Units	Entry Price	Exit Price	Close Date/Time	Pips W/L	Profit/ Loss	New Balance

TRADE SETUP NOTES:

ADDITIONAL NOTES:

Order Date/Time	Pair	Order Ticket #	Buy/ Sell	Lots/ Units	Entry Price	Exit Price	Close Date/Time	Pips W/L	Profit/ Loss	New Balance

TRADE SETUP NOTES:

ADDITIONAL NOTES:

Order Date/Time	Pair	Order Ticket #	Buy/ Sell	Lots/ Units	Entry Price	Exit Price	Close Date/Time	Pips W/L	Profit/ Loss	New Balance

TRADE SETUP NOTES:

ADDITIONAL NOTES:

Order Date/Time	Pair	Order Ticket #	Buy/ Sell	Lots/ Units	Entry Price	Exit Price	Close Date/Time	Pips W/L	Profit/ Loss	New Balance

TRADE SETUP NOTES:

ADDITIONAL NOTES:

Order Date/Time	Pair	Order Ticket #	Buy/ Sell	Lots/ Units	Entry Price	Exit Price	Close Date/Time	Pips W/L	Profit/ Loss	New Balance

TRADE SETUP NOTES:

ADDITIONAL NOTES:

Order Date/Time	Pair	Order Ticket #	Buy/ Sell	Lots/ Units	Entry Price	Exit Price	Close Date/Time	Pips W/L	Profit/ Loss	New Balance

TRADE SETUP NOTES:

ADDITIONAL NOTES:

TRADING LOG

Order Date/Time	Pair	Order Ticket #	Buy/ Sell	Lots/ Units	Entry Price	Exit Price	Close Date/Time	Pips W/L	Profit/ Loss	New Balance

TRADE SETUP NOTES:

ADDITIONAL NOTES:

Order Date/Time	Pair	Order Ticket #	Buy/ Sell	Lots/ Units	Entry Price	Exit Price	Close Date/Time	Pips W/L	Profit/ Loss	New Balance

TRADE SETUP NOTES:

ADDITIONAL NOTES:

Order Date/Time	Pair	Order Ticket #	Buy/ Sell	Lots/ Units	Entry Price	Exit Price	Close Date/Time	Pips W/L	Profit/ Loss	New Balance

TRADE SETUP NOTES:

ADDITIONAL NOTES:

Order Date/Time	Pair	Order Ticket #	Buy/ Sell	Lots/ Units	Entry Price	Exit Price	Close Date/Time	Pips W/L	Profit/ Loss	New Balance

TRADE SETUP NOTES:

ADDITIONAL NOTES:

Order Date/Time	Pair	Order Ticket #	Buy/ Sell	Lots/ Units	Entry Price	Exit Price	Close Date/Time	Pips W/L	Profit/ Loss	New Balance

TRADE SETUP NOTES:

ADDITIONAL NOTES:

Order Date/Time	Pair	Order Ticket #	Buy/ Sell	Lots/ Units	Entry Price	Exit Price	Close Date/Time	Pips W/L	Profit/ Loss	New Balance

TRADE SETUP NOTES:

ADDITIONAL NOTES:

TRADING LOG

Order Date/Time	Pair	Order Ticket #	Buy/ Sell	Lots/ Units	Entry Price	Exit Price	Close Date/Time	Pips W/L	Profit/ Loss	New Balance

TRADE SETUP NOTES:

ADDITIONAL NOTES:

Order Date/Time	Pair	Order Ticket #	Buy/ Sell	Lots/ Units	Entry Price	Exit Price	Close Date/Time	Pips W/L	Profit/ Loss	New Balance

TRADE SETUP NOTES:

ADDITIONAL NOTES:

Order Date/Time	Pair	Order Ticket #	Buy/ Sell	Lots/ Units	Entry Price	Exit Price	Close Date/Time	Pips W/L	Profit/ Loss	New Balance

TRADE SETUP NOTES:

ADDITIONAL NOTES:

Order Date/Time	Pair	Order Ticket #	Buy/ Sell	Lots/ Units	Entry Price	Exit Price	Close Date/Time	Pips W/L	Profit/ Loss	New Balance

TRADE SETUP NOTES:

ADDITIONAL NOTES:

Order Date/Time	Pair	Order Ticket #	Buy/ Sell	Lots/ Units	Entry Price	Exit Price	Close Date/Time	Pips W/L	Profit/ Loss	New Balance

TRADE SETUP NOTES:

ADDITIONAL NOTES:

Order Date/Time	Pair	Order Ticket #	Buy/ Sell	Lots/ Units	Entry Price	Exit Price	Close Date/Time	Pips W/L	Profit/ Loss	New Balance

TRADE SETUP NOTES:

ADDITIONAL NOTES:

Order Date/Time	Pair	Order Ticket #	Buy/ Sell	Lots/ Units	Entry Price	Exit Price	Close Date/Time	Pips W/L	Profit/ Loss	New Balance

TRADE SETUP NOTES:

ADDITIONAL NOTES:

TRADING LOG

Order Date/Time	Pair	Order Ticket #	Buy/ Sell	Lots/ Units	Entry Price	Exit Price	Close Date/Time	Pips W/L	Profit/ Loss	New Balance

TRADE SETUP NOTES:

ADDITIONAL NOTES:

Order Date/Time	Pair	Order Ticket #	Buy/ Sell	Lots/ Units	Entry Price	Exit Price	Close Date/Time	Pips W/L	Profit/ Loss	New Balance

TRADE SETUP NOTES:

ADDITIONAL NOTES:

Order Date/Time	Pair	Order Ticket #	Buy/ Sell	Lots/ Units	Entry Price	Exit Price	Close Date/Time	Pips W/L	Profit/ Loss	New Balance

TRADE SETUP NOTES:

ADDITIONAL NOTES:

Order Date/Time	Pair	Order Ticket #	Buy/ Sell	Lots/ Units	Entry Price	Exit Price	Close Date/Time	Pips W/L	Profit/ Loss	New Balance

TRADE SETUP NOTES:

ADDITIONAL NOTES:

Order Date/Time	Pair	Order Ticket #	Buy/ Sell	Lots/ Units	Entry Price	Exit Price	Close Date/Time	Pips W/L	Profit/ Loss	New Balance

TRADE SETUP NOTES:

ADDITIONAL NOTES:

Order Date/Time	Pair	Order Ticket #	Buy/ Sell	Lots/ Units	Entry Price	Exit Price	Close Date/Time	Pips W/L	Profit/ Loss	New Balance

TRADE SETUP NOTES:

ADDITIONAL NOTES:

TRADING LOG

Order Date/Time	Pair	Order Ticket #	Buy/ Sell	Lots/ Units	Entry Price	Exit Price	Close Date/Time	Pips W/L	Profit/ Loss	New Balance

TRADE SETUP NOTES:

ADDITIONAl NOTES:

Order Date/Time	Pair	Order Ticket #	Buy/ Sell	Lots/ Units	Entry Price	Exit Price	Close Date/Time	Pips W/L	Profit/ Loss	New Balance

TRADE SETUP NOTES:

ADDITIONAl NOTES:

Order Date/Time	Pair	Order Ticket #	Buy/ Sell	Lots/ Units	Entry Price	Exit Price	Close Date/Time	Pips W/L	Profit/ Loss	New Balance

TRADE SETUP NOTES:

ADDITIONAl NOTES:

Order Date/Time	Pair	Order Ticket #	Buy/ Sell	Lots/ Units	Entry Price	Exit Price	Close Date/Time	Pips W/L	Profit/ Loss	New Balance

TRADE SETUP NOTES:

ADDITIONAl NOTES:

Order Date/Time	Pair	Order Ticket #	Buy/ Sell	Lots/ Units	Entry Price	Exit Price	Close Date/Time	Pips W/L	Profit/ Loss	New Balance

TRADE SETUP NOTES:

ADDITIONAl NOTES:

Order Date/Time	Pair	Order Ticket #	Buy/ Sell	Lots/ Units	Entry Price	Exit Price	Close Date/Time	Pips W/L	Profit/ Loss	New Balance

TRADE SETUP NOTES:

ADDITIONAl NOTES:

Order Date/Time	Pair	Order Ticket #	Buy/ Sell	Lots/ Units	Entry Price	Exit Price	Close Date/Time	Pips W/L	Profit/ Loss	New Balance

TRADE SETUP NOTES:

ADDITIONAl NOTES:

TRADING LOG

Order Date/Time	Pair	Order Ticket #	Buy/ Sell	Lots/ Units	Entry Price	Exit Price	Close Date/Time	Pips W/L	Profit/ Loss	New Balance

TRADE SETUP NOTES:

ADDITIONAL NOTES:

Order Date/Time	Pair	Order Ticket #	Buy/ Sell	Lots/ Units	Entry Price	Exit Price	Close Date/Time	Pips W/L	Profit/ Loss	New Balance

TRADE SETUP NOTES:

ADDITIONAL NOTES:

Order Date/Time	Pair	Order Ticket #	Buy/ Sell	Lots/ Units	Entry Price	Exit Price	Close Date/Time	Pips W/L	Profit/ Loss	New Balance

TRADE SETUP NOTES:

ADDITIONAL NOTES:

Order Date/Time	Pair	Order Ticket #	Buy/ Sell	Lots/ Units	Entry Price	Exit Price	Close Date/Time	Pips W/L	Profit/ Loss	New Balance

TRADE SETUP NOTES:

ADDITIONAL NOTES:

Order Date/Time	Pair	Order Ticket #	Buy/ Sell	Lots/ Units	Entry Price	Exit Price	Close Date/Time	Pips W/L	Profit/ Loss	New Balance

TRADE SETUP NOTES:

ADDITIONAL NOTES:

Order Date/Time	Pair	Order Ticket #	Buy/ Sell	Lots/ Units	Entry Price	Exit Price	Close Date/Time	Pips W/L	Profit/ Loss	New Balance

TRADE SETUP NOTES:

ADDITIONAL NOTES:

TRADING LOG

Order Date/Time	Pair	Order Ticket #	Buy/ Sell	Lots/ Units	Entry Price	Exit Price	Close Date/Time	Pips W/L	Profit/ Loss	New Balance

TRADE SETUP NOTES:

ADDITIONAL NOTES:

Order Date/Time	Pair	Order Ticket #	Buy/ Sell	Lots/ Units	Entry Price	Exit Price	Close Date/Time	Pips W/L	Profit/ Loss	New Balance

TRADE SETUP NOTES:

ADDITIONAL NOTES:

Order Date/Time	Pair	Order Ticket #	Buy/ Sell	Lots/ Units	Entry Price	Exit Price	Close Date/Time	Pips W/L	Profit/ Loss	New Balance

TRADE SETUP NOTES:

ADDITIONAL NOTES:

Order Date/Time	Pair	Order Ticket #	Buy/ Sell	Lots/ Units	Entry Price	Exit Price	Close Date/Time	Pips W/L	Profit/ Loss	New Balance

TRADE SETUP NOTES:

ADDITIONAL NOTES:

Order Date/Time	Pair	Order Ticket #	Buy/ Sell	Lots/ Units	Entry Price	Exit Price	Close Date/Time	Pips W/L	Profit/ Loss	New Balance

TRADE SETUP NOTES:

ADDITIONAL NOTES:

Order Date/Time	Pair	Order Ticket #	Buy/ Sell	Lots/ Units	Entry Price	Exit Price	Close Date/Time	Pips W/L	Profit/ Loss	New Balance

TRADE SETUP NOTES:

ADDITIONAL NOTES:

Order Date/Time	Pair	Order Ticket #	Buy/ Sell	Lots/ Units	Entry Price	Exit Price	Close Date/Time	Pips W/L	Profit/ Loss	New Balance

TRADE SETUP NOTES:

ADDITIONAL NOTES:

TRADING LOG

Order Date/Time	Pair	Order Ticket #	Buy/ Sell	Lots/ Units	Entry Price	Exit Price	Close Date/Time	Pips W/L	Profit/ Loss	New Balance

TRADE SETUP NOTES:

ADDITIONAL NOTES:

Order Date/Time	Pair	Order Ticket #	Buy/ Sell	Lots/ Units	Entry Price	Exit Price	Close Date/Time	Pips W/L	Profit/ Loss	New Balance

TRADE SETUP NOTES:

ADDITIONAL NOTES:

Order Date/Time	Pair	Order Ticket #	Buy/ Sell	Lots/ Units	Entry Price	Exit Price	Close Date/Time	Pips W/L	Profit/ Loss	New Balance

TRADE SETUP NOTES:

ADDITIONAL NOTES:

Order Date/Time	Pair	Order Ticket #	Buy/ Sell	Lots/ Units	Entry Price	Exit Price	Close Date/Time	Pips W/L	Profit/ Loss	New Balance

TRADE SETUP NOTES:

ADDITIONAL NOTES:

Order Date/Time	Pair	Order Ticket #	Buy/ Sell	Lots/ Units	Entry Price	Exit Price	Close Date/Time	Pips W/L	Profit/ Loss	New Balance

TRADE SETUP NOTES:

ADDITIONAL NOTES:

Order Date/Time	Pair	Order Ticket #	Buy/ Sell	Lots/ Units	Entry Price	Exit Price	Close Date/Time	Pips W/L	Profit/ Loss	New Balance

TRADE SETUP NOTES:

ADDITIONAL NOTES:

TRADING LOG

Order Date/Time	Pair	Order Ticket #	Buy/ Sell	Lots/ Units	Entry Price	Exit Price	Close Date/Time	Pips W/L	Profit/ Loss	New Balance

TRADE SETUP NOTES:

ADDITIONAL NOTES:

Order Date/Time	Pair	Order Ticket #	Buy/ Sell	Lots/ Units	Entry Price	Exit Price	Close Date/Time	Pips W/L	Profit/ Loss	New Balance

TRADE SETUP NOTES:

ADDITIONAL NOTES:

Order Date/Time	Pair	Order Ticket #	Buy/ Sell	Lots/ Units	Entry Price	Exit Price	Close Date/Time	Pips W/L	Profit/ Loss	New Balance

TRADE SETUP NOTES:

ADDITIONAL NOTES:

Order Date/Time	Pair	Order Ticket #	Buy/ Sell	Lots/ Units	Entry Price	Exit Price	Close Date/Time	Pips W/L	Profit/ Loss	New Balance

TRADE SETUP NOTES:

ADDITIONAL NOTES:

Order Date/Time	Pair	Order Ticket #	Buy/ Sell	Lots/ Units	Entry Price	Exit Price	Close Date/Time	Pips W/L	Profit/ Loss	New Balance

TRADE SETUP NOTES:

ADDITIONAL NOTES:

Order Date/Time	Pair	Order Ticket #	Buy/ Sell	Lots/ Units	Entry Price	Exit Price	Close Date/Time	Pips W/L	Profit/ Loss	New Balance

TRADE SETUP NOTES:

ADDITIONAL NOTES:

Order Date/Time	Pair	Order Ticket #	Buy/ Sell	Lots/ Units	Entry Price	Exit Price	Close Date/Time	Pips W/L	Profit/ Loss	New Balance

TRADE SETUP NOTES:

ADDITIONAL NOTES:

TRADING LOG

Order Date/Time	Pair	Order Ticket #	Buy/ Sell	Lots/ Units	Entry Price	Exit Price	Close Date/Time	Pips W/L	Profit/ Loss	New Balance

TRADE SETUP NOTES:

ADDITIONAL NOTES:

Order Date/Time	Pair	Order Ticket #	Buy/ Sell	Lots/ Units	Entry Price	Exit Price	Close Date/Time	Pips W/L	Profit/ Loss	New Balance

TRADE SETUP NOTES:

ADDITIONAL NOTES:

Order Date/Time	Pair	Order Ticket #	Buy/ Sell	Lots/ Units	Entry Price	Exit Price	Close Date/Time	Pips W/L	Profit/ Loss	New Balance

TRADE SETUP NOTES:

ADDITIONAL NOTES:

Order Date/Time	Pair	Order Ticket #	Buy/ Sell	Lots/ Units	Entry Price	Exit Price	Close Date/Time	Pips W/L	Profit/ Loss	New Balance

TRADE SETUP NOTES:

ADDITIONAL NOTES:

Order Date/Time	Pair	Order Ticket #	Buy/ Sell	Lots/ Units	Entry Price	Exit Price	Close Date/Time	Pips W/L	Profit/ Loss	New Balance

TRADE SETUP NOTES:

ADDITIONAL NOTES:

Order Date/Time	Pair	Order Ticket #	Buy/ Sell	Lots/ Units	Entry Price	Exit Price	Close Date/Time	Pips W/L	Profit/ Loss	New Balance

TRADE SETUP NOTES:

ADDITIONAL NOTES:

TRADING LOG

Order Date/Time	Pair	Order Ticket #	Buy/ Sell	Lots/ Units	Entry Price	Exit Price	Close Date/Time	Pips W/L	Profit/ Loss	New Balance

TRADE SETUP NOTES:

ADDITIONAL NOTES:

Order Date/Time	Pair	Order Ticket #	Buy/ Sell	Lots/ Units	Entry Price	Exit Price	Close Date/Time	Pips W/L	Profit/ Loss	New Balance

TRADE SETUP NOTES:

ADDITIONAL NOTES:

Order Date/Time	Pair	Order Ticket #	Buy/ Sell	Lots/ Units	Entry Price	Exit Price	Close Date/Time	Pips W/L	Profit/ Loss	New Balance

TRADE SETUP NOTES:

ADDITIONAL NOTES:

Order Date/Time	Pair	Order Ticket #	Buy/ Sell	Lots/ Units	Entry Price	Exit Price	Close Date/Time	Pips W/L	Profit/ Loss	New Balance

TRADE SETUP NOTES:

ADDITIONAL NOTES:

Order Date/Time	Pair	Order Ticket #	Buy/ Sell	Lots/ Units	Entry Price	Exit Price	Close Date/Time	Pips W/L	Profit/ Loss	New Balance

TRADE SETUP NOTES:

ADDITIONAL NOTES:

Order Date/Time	Pair	Order Ticket #	Buy/ Sell	Lots/ Units	Entry Price	Exit Price	Close Date/Time	Pips W/L	Profit/ Loss	New Balance

TRADE SETUP NOTES:

ADDITIONAL NOTES:

Order Date/Time	Pair	Order Ticket #	Buy/ Sell	Lots/ Units	Entry Price	Exit Price	Close Date/Time	Pips W/L	Profit/ Loss	New Balance

TRADE SETUP NOTES:

ADDITIONAL NOTES:

TRADING LOG

Order Date/Time	Pair	Order Ticket #	Buy/ Sell	Lots/ Units	Entry Price	Exit Price	Close Date/Time	Pips W/L	Profit/ Loss	New Balance

TRADE SETUP NOTES:

ADDITIONAL NOTES:

Order Date/Time	Pair	Order Ticket #	Buy/ Sell	Lots/ Units	Entry Price	Exit Price	Close Date/Time	Pips W/L	Profit/ Loss	New Balance

TRADE SETUP NOTES:

ADDITIONAL NOTES:

Order Date/Time	Pair	Order Ticket #	Buy/ Sell	Lots/ Units	Entry Price	Exit Price	Close Date/Time	Pips W/L	Profit/ Loss	New Balance

TRADE SETUP NOTES:

ADDITIONAL NOTES:

Order Date/Time	Pair	Order Ticket #	Buy/ Sell	Lots/ Units	Entry Price	Exit Price	Close Date/Time	Pips W/L	Profit/ Loss	New Balance

TRADE SETUP NOTES:

ADDITIONAL NOTES:

Order Date/Time	Pair	Order Ticket #	Buy/ Sell	Lots/ Units	Entry Price	Exit Price	Close Date/Time	Pips W/L	Profit/ Loss	New Balance

TRADE SETUP NOTES:

ADDITIONAL NOTES:

Order Date/Time	Pair	Order Ticket #	Buy/ Sell	Lots/ Units	Entry Price	Exit Price	Close Date/Time	Pips W/L	Profit/ Loss	New Balance

TRADE SETUP NOTES:

ADDITIONAL NOTES:

TRADING LOG

Order Date/Time	Pair	Order Ticket #	Buy/ Sell	Lots/ Units	Entry Price	Exit Price	Close Date/Time	Pips W/L	Profit/ Loss	New Balance

TRADE SETUP NOTES:

ADDITIONAL NOTES:

Order Date/Time	Pair	Order Ticket #	Buy/ Sell	Lots/ Units	Entry Price	Exit Price	Close Date/Time	Pips W/L	Profit/ Loss	New Balance

TRADE SETUP NOTES:

ADDITIONAL NOTES:

Order Date/Time	Pair	Order Ticket #	Buy/ Sell	Lots/ Units	Entry Price	Exit Price	Close Date/Time	Pips W/L	Profit/ Loss	New Balance

TRADE SETUP NOTES:

ADDITIONAL NOTES:

Order Date/Time	Pair	Order Ticket #	Buy/ Sell	Lots/ Units	Entry Price	Exit Price	Close Date/Time	Pips W/L	Profit/ Loss	New Balance

TRADE SETUP NOTES:

ADDITIONAL NOTES:

Order Date/Time	Pair	Order Ticket #	Buy/ Sell	Lots/ Units	Entry Price	Exit Price	Close Date/Time	Pips W/L	Profit/ Loss	New Balance

TRADE SETUP NOTES:

ADDITIONAL NOTES:

Order Date/Time	Pair	Order Ticket #	Buy/ Sell	Lots/ Units	Entry Price	Exit Price	Close Date/Time	Pips W/L	Profit/ Loss	New Balance

TRADE SETUP NOTES:

ADDITIONAL NOTES:

Order Date/Time	Pair	Order Ticket #	Buy/ Sell	Lots/ Units	Entry Price	Exit Price	Close Date/Time	Pips W/L	Profit/ Loss	New Balance

TRADE SETUP NOTES:

ADDITIONAL NOTES:

TRADING LOG

Order Date/Time	Pair	Order Ticket #	Buy/ Sell	Lots/ Units	Entry Price	Exit Price	Close Date/Time	Pips W/L	Profit/ Loss	New Balance

TRADE SETUP NOTES:

ADDITIONAL NOTES:

Order Date/Time	Pair	Order Ticket #	Buy/ Sell	Lots/ Units	Entry Price	Exit Price	Close Date/Time	Pips W/L	Profit/ Loss	New Balance

TRADE SETUP NOTES:

ADDITIONAL NOTES:

Order Date/Time	Pair	Order Ticket #	Buy/ Sell	Lots/ Units	Entry Price	Exit Price	Close Date/Time	Pips W/L	Profit/ Loss	New Balance

TRADE SETUP NOTES:

ADDITIONAL NOTES:

Order Date/Time	Pair	Order Ticket #	Buy/ Sell	Lots/ Units	Entry Price	Exit Price	Close Date/Time	Pips W/L	Profit/ Loss	New Balance

TRADE SETUP NOTES:

ADDITIONAL NOTES:

Order Date/Time	Pair	Order Ticket #	Buy/ Sell	Lots/ Units	Entry Price	Exit Price	Close Date/Time	Pips W/L	Profit/ Loss	New Balance

TRADE SETUP NOTES:

ADDITIONAL NOTES:

Order Date/Time	Pair	Order Ticket #	Buy/ Sell	Lots/ Units	Entry Price	Exit Price	Close Date/Time	Pips W/L	Profit/ Loss	New Balance

TRADE SETUP NOTES:

ADDITIONAL NOTES:

TRADING LOG

Order Date/Time	Pair	Order Ticket #	Buy/ Sell	Lots/ Units	Entry Price	Exit Price	Close Date/Time	Pips W/L	Profit/ Loss	New Balance

TRADE SETUP NOTES:

ADDITIONAL NOTES:

Order Date/Time	Pair	Order Ticket #	Buy/ Sell	Lots/ Units	Entry Price	Exit Price	Close Date/Time	Pips W/L	Profit/ Loss	New Balance

TRADE SETUP NOTES:

ADDITIONAL NOTES:

Order Date/Time	Pair	Order Ticket #	Buy/ Sell	Lots/ Units	Entry Price	Exit Price	Close Date/Time	Pips W/L	Profit/ Loss	New Balance

TRADE SETUP NOTES:

ADDITIONAL NOTES:

Order Date/Time	Pair	Order Ticket #	Buy/ Sell	Lots/ Units	Entry Price	Exit Price	Close Date/Time	Pips W/L	Profit/ Loss	New Balance

TRADE SETUP NOTES:

ADDITIONAL NOTES:

Order Date/Time	Pair	Order Ticket #	Buy/ Sell	Lots/ Units	Entry Price	Exit Price	Close Date/Time	Pips W/L	Profit/ Loss	New Balance

TRADE SETUP NOTES:

ADDITIONAL NOTES:

Order Date/Time	Pair	Order Ticket #	Buy/ Sell	Lots/ Units	Entry Price	Exit Price	Close Date/Time	Pips W/L	Profit/ Loss	New Balance

TRADE SETUP NOTES:

ADDITIONAL NOTES:

Order Date/Time	Pair	Order Ticket #	Buy/ Sell	Lots/ Units	Entry Price	Exit Price	Close Date/Time	Pips W/L	Profit/ Loss	New Balance

TRADE SETUP NOTES:

ADDITIONAL NOTES:

TRADING LOG

Order Date/Time	Pair	Order Ticket #	Buy/ Sell	Lots/ Units	Entry Price	Exit Price	Close Date/Time	Pips W/L	Profit/ Loss	New Balance

TRADE SETUP NOTES:

ADDITIONAL NOTES:

Order Date/Time	Pair	Order Ticket #	Buy/ Sell	Lots/ Units	Entry Price	Exit Price	Close Date/Time	Pips W/L	Profit/ Loss	New Balance

TRADE SETUP NOTES:

ADDITIONAL NOTES:

Order Date/Time	Pair	Order Ticket #	Buy/ Sell	Lots/ Units	Entry Price	Exit Price	Close Date/Time	Pips W/L	Profit/ Loss	New Balance

TRADE SETUP NOTES:

ADDITIONAL NOTES:

Order Date/Time	Pair	Order Ticket #	Buy/ Sell	Lots/ Units	Entry Price	Exit Price	Close Date/Time	Pips W/L	Profit/ Loss	New Balance

TRADE SETUP NOTES:

ADDITIONAL NOTES:

Order Date/Time	Pair	Order Ticket #	Buy/ Sell	Lots/ Units	Entry Price	Exit Price	Close Date/Time	Pips W/L	Profit/ Loss	New Balance

TRADE SETUP NOTES:

ADDITIONAL NOTES:

Order Date/Time	Pair	Order Ticket #	Buy/ Sell	Lots/ Units	Entry Price	Exit Price	Close Date/Time	Pips W/L	Profit/ Loss	New Balance

TRADE SETUP NOTES:

ADDITIONAL NOTES:

TRADING LOG

Order Date/Time	Pair	Order Ticket #	Buy/ Sell	Lots/ Units	Entry Price	Exit Price	Close Date/Time	Pips W/L	Profit/ Loss	New Balance

TRADE SETUP NOTES:

ADDITIONAl NOTES:

Order Date/Time	Pair	Order Ticket #	Buy/ Sell	Lots/ Units	Entry Price	Exit Price	Close Date/Time	Pips W/L	Profit/ Loss	New Balance

TRADE SETUP NOTES:

ADDITIONAl NOTES:

Order Date/Time	Pair	Order Ticket #	Buy/ Sell	Lots/ Units	Entry Price	Exit Price	Close Date/Time	Pips W/L	Profit/ Loss	New Balance

TRADE SETUP NOTES:

ADDITIONAl NOTES:

Order Date/Time	Pair	Order Ticket #	Buy/ Sell	Lots/ Units	Entry Price	Exit Price	Close Date/Time	Pips W/L	Profit/ Loss	New Balance

TRADE SETUP NOTES:

ADDITIONAl NOTES:

Order Date/Time	Pair	Order Ticket #	Buy/ Sell	Lots/ Units	Entry Price	Exit Price	Close Date/Time	Pips W/L	Profit/ Loss	New Balance

TRADE SETUP NOTES:

ADDITIONAl NOTES:

Order Date/Time	Pair	Order Ticket #	Buy/ Sell	Lots/ Units	Entry Price	Exit Price	Close Date/Time	Pips W/L	Profit/ Loss	New Balance

TRADE SETUP NOTES:

ADDITIONAl NOTES:

TRADING LOG

Order Date/Time	Pair	Order Ticket #	Buy/ Sell	Lots/ Units	Entry Price	Exit Price	Close Date/Time	Pips W/L	Profit/ Loss	New Balance

TRADE SETUP NOTES:

ADDITIONAL NOTES:

Order Date/Time	Pair	Order Ticket #	Buy/ Sell	Lots/ Units	Entry Price	Exit Price	Close Date/Time	Pips W/L	Profit/ Loss	New Balance

TRADE SETUP NOTES:

ADDITIONAL NOTES:

Order Date/Time	Pair	Order Ticket #	Buy/ Sell	Lots/ Units	Entry Price	Exit Price	Close Date/Time	Pips W/L	Profit/ Loss	New Balance

TRADE SETUP NOTES:

ADDITIONAL NOTES:

Order Date/Time	Pair	Order Ticket #	Buy/ Sell	Lots/ Units	Entry Price	Exit Price	Close Date/Time	Pips W/L	Profit/ Loss	New Balance

TRADE SETUP NOTES:

ADDITIONAL NOTES:

Order Date/Time	Pair	Order Ticket #	Buy/ Sell	Lots/ Units	Entry Price	Exit Price	Close Date/Time	Pips W/L	Profit/ Loss	New Balance

TRADE SETUP NOTES:

ADDITIONAL NOTES:

Order Date/Time	Pair	Order Ticket #	Buy/ Sell	Lots/ Units	Entry Price	Exit Price	Close Date/Time	Pips W/L	Profit/ Loss	New Balance

TRADE SETUP NOTES:

ADDITIONAL NOTES:

TRADING LOG

Order Date/Time	Pair	Order Ticket #	Buy/ Sell	Lots/ Units	Entry Price	Exit Price	Close Date/Time	Pips W/L	Profit/ Loss	New Balance

TRADE SETUP NOTES:

ADDITIONAL NOTES:

Order Date/Time	Pair	Order Ticket #	Buy/ Sell	Lots/ Units	Entry Price	Exit Price	Close Date/Time	Pips W/L	Profit/ Loss	New Balance

TRADE SETUP NOTES:

ADDITIONAL NOTES:

Order Date/Time	Pair	Order Ticket #	Buy/ Sell	Lots/ Units	Entry Price	Exit Price	Close Date/Time	Pips W/L	Profit/ Loss	New Balance

TRADE SETUP NOTES:

ADDITIONAL NOTES:

Order Date/Time	Pair	Order Ticket #	Buy/ Sell	Lots/ Units	Entry Price	Exit Price	Close Date/Time	Pips W/L	Profit/ Loss	New Balance

TRADE SETUP NOTES:

ADDITIONAL NOTES:

Order Date/Time	Pair	Order Ticket #	Buy/ Sell	Lots/ Units	Entry Price	Exit Price	Close Date/Time	Pips W/L	Profit/ Loss	New Balance

TRADE SETUP NOTES:

ADDITIONAL NOTES:

Order Date/Time	Pair	Order Ticket #	Buy/ Sell	Lots/ Units	Entry Price	Exit Price	Close Date/Time	Pips W/L	Profit/ Loss	New Balance

TRADE SETUP NOTES:

ADDITIONAL NOTES:

TRADING LOG

Order Date/Time	Pair	Order Ticket #	Buy/ Sell	Lots/ Units	Entry Price	Exit Price	Close Date/Time	Pips W/L	Profit/ Loss	New Balance

TRADE SETUP NOTES:

ADDITIONAL NOTES:

Order Date/Time	Pair	Order Ticket #	Buy/ Sell	Lots/ Units	Entry Price	Exit Price	Close Date/Time	Pips W/L	Profit/ Loss	New Balance

TRADE SETUP NOTES:

ADDITIONAL NOTES:

Order Date/Time	Pair	Order Ticket #	Buy/ Sell	Lots/ Units	Entry Price	Exit Price	Close Date/Time	Pips W/L	Profit/ Loss	New Balance

TRADE SETUP NOTES:

ADDITIONAL NOTES:

Order Date/Time	Pair	Order Ticket #	Buy/ Sell	Lots/ Units	Entry Price	Exit Price	Close Date/Time	Pips W/L	Profit/ Loss	New Balance

TRADE SETUP NOTES:

ADDITIONAL NOTES:

Order Date/Time	Pair	Order Ticket #	Buy/ Sell	Lots/ Units	Entry Price	Exit Price	Close Date/Time	Pips W/L	Profit/ Loss	New Balance

TRADE SETUP NOTES:

ADDITIONAL NOTES:

Order Date/Time	Pair	Order Ticket #	Buy/ Sell	Lots/ Units	Entry Price	Exit Price	Close Date/Time	Pips W/L	Profit/ Loss	New Balance

TRADE SETUP NOTES:

ADDITIONAL NOTES:

TRADING LOG

Order Date/Time	Pair	Order Ticket #	Buy/ Sell	Lots/ Units	Entry Price	Exit Price	Close Date/Time	Pips W/L	Profit/ Loss	New Balance

TRADE SETUP NOTES:

ADDITIONAl NOTES:

Order Date/Time	Pair	Order Ticket #	Buy/ Sell	Lots/ Units	Entry Price	Exit Price	Close Date/Time	Pips W/L	Profit/ Loss	New Balance

TRADE SETUP NOTES:

ADDITIONAl NOTES:

Order Date/Time	Pair	Order Ticket #	Buy/ Sell	Lots/ Units	Entry Price	Exit Price	Close Date/Time	Pips W/L	Profit/ Loss	New Balance

TRADE SETUP NOTES:

ADDITIONAl NOTES:

Order Date/Time	Pair	Order Ticket #	Buy/ Sell	Lots/ Units	Entry Price	Exit Price	Close Date/Time	Pips W/L	Profit/ Loss	New Balance

TRADE SETUP NOTES:

ADDITIONAl NOTES:

Order Date/Time	Pair	Order Ticket #	Buy/ Sell	Lots/ Units	Entry Price	Exit Price	Close Date/Time	Pips W/L	Profit/ Loss	New Balance

TRADE SETUP NOTES:

ADDITIONAl NOTES:

Order Date/Time	Pair	Order Ticket #	Buy/ Sell	Lots/ Units	Entry Price	Exit Price	Close Date/Time	Pips W/L	Profit/ Loss	New Balance

TRADE SETUP NOTES:

ADDITIONAl NOTES:

Order Date/Time	Pair	Order Ticket #	Buy/ Sell	Lots/ Units	Entry Price	Exit Price	Close Date/Time	Pips W/L	Profit/ Loss	New Balance

TRADE SETUP NOTES:

ADDITIONAl NOTES:

TRADING LOG

Order Date/Time	Pair	Order Ticket #	Buy/ Sell	Lots/ Units	Entry Price	Exit Price	Close Date/Time	Pips W/L	Profit/ Loss	New Balance

TRADE SETUP NOTES:

ADDITIONAL NOTES:

Order Date/Time	Pair	Order Ticket #	Buy/ Sell	Lots/ Units	Entry Price	Exit Price	Close Date/Time	Pips W/L	Profit/ Loss	New Balance

TRADE SETUP NOTES:

ADDITIONAL NOTES:

Order Date/Time	Pair	Order Ticket #	Buy/ Sell	Lots/ Units	Entry Price	Exit Price	Close Date/Time	Pips W/L	Profit/ Loss	New Balance

TRADE SETUP NOTES:

ADDITIONAL NOTES:

Order Date/Time	Pair	Order Ticket #	Buy/ Sell	Lots/ Units	Entry Price	Exit Price	Close Date/Time	Pips W/L	Profit/ Loss	New Balance

TRADE SETUP NOTES:

ADDITIONAL NOTES:

Order Date/Time	Pair	Order Ticket #	Buy/ Sell	Lots/ Units	Entry Price	Exit Price	Close Date/Time	Pips W/L	Profit/ Loss	New Balance

TRADE SETUP NOTES:

ADDITIONAL NOTES:

Order Date/Time	Pair	Order Ticket #	Buy/ Sell	Lots/ Units	Entry Price	Exit Price	Close Date/Time	Pips W/L	Profit/ Loss	New Balance

TRADE SETUP NOTES:

ADDITIONAL NOTES:

TRADING LOG

Order Date/Time	Pair	Order Ticket #	Buy/ Sell	Lots/ Units	Entry Price	Exit Price	Close Date/Time	Pips W/L	Profit/ Loss	New Balance

TRADE SETUP NOTES:

ADDITIONAL NOTES:

Order Date/Time	Pair	Order Ticket #	Buy/ Sell	Lots/ Units	Entry Price	Exit Price	Close Date/Time	Pips W/L	Profit/ Loss	New Balance

TRADE SETUP NOTES:

ADDITIONAL NOTES:

Order Date/Time	Pair	Order Ticket #	Buy/ Sell	Lots/ Units	Entry Price	Exit Price	Close Date/Time	Pips W/L	Profit/ Loss	New Balance

TRADE SETUP NOTES:

ADDITIONAL NOTES:

Order Date/Time	Pair	Order Ticket #	Buy/ Sell	Lots/ Units	Entry Price	Exit Price	Close Date/Time	Pips W/L	Profit/ Loss	New Balance

TRADE SETUP NOTES:

ADDITIONAL NOTES:

Order Date/Time	Pair	Order Ticket #	Buy/ Sell	Lots/ Units	Entry Price	Exit Price	Close Date/Time	Pips W/L	Profit/ Loss	New Balance

TRADE SETUP NOTES:

ADDITIONAL NOTES:

Order Date/Time	Pair	Order Ticket #	Buy/ Sell	Lots/ Units	Entry Price	Exit Price	Close Date/Time	Pips W/L	Profit/ Loss	New Balance

TRADE SETUP NOTES:

ADDITIONAL NOTES:

Order Date/Time	Pair	Order Ticket #	Buy/ Sell	Lots/ Units	Entry Price	Exit Price	Close Date/Time	Pips W/L	Profit/ Loss	New Balance

TRADE SETUP NOTES:

ADDITIONAL NOTES:

TRADING LOG

Order Date/Time	Pair	Order Ticket #	Buy/ Sell	Lots/ Units	Entry Price	Exit Price	Close Date/Time	Pips W/L	Profit/ Loss	New Balance

TRADE SETUP NOTES:

ADDITIONAL NOTES:

Order Date/Time	Pair	Order Ticket #	Buy/ Sell	Lots/ Units	Entry Price	Exit Price	Close Date/Time	Pips W/L	Profit/ Loss	New Balance

TRADE SETUP NOTES:

ADDITIONAL NOTES:

Order Date/Time	Pair	Order Ticket #	Buy/ Sell	Lots/ Units	Entry Price	Exit Price	Close Date/Time	Pips W/L	Profit/ Loss	New Balance

TRADE SETUP NOTES:

ADDITIONAL NOTES:

Order Date/Time	Pair	Order Ticket #	Buy/ Sell	Lots/ Units	Entry Price	Exit Price	Close Date/Time	Pips W/L	Profit/ Loss	New Balance

TRADE SETUP NOTES:

ADDITIONAL NOTES:

Order Date/Time	Pair	Order Ticket #	Buy/ Sell	Lots/ Units	Entry Price	Exit Price	Close Date/Time	Pips W/L	Profit/ Loss	New Balance

TRADE SETUP NOTES:

ADDITIONAL NOTES:

Order Date/Time	Pair	Order Ticket #	Buy/ Sell	Lots/ Units	Entry Price	Exit Price	Close Date/Time	Pips W/L	Profit/ Loss	New Balance

TRADE SETUP NOTES:

ADDITIONAL NOTES:

TRADING LOG

Order Date/Time	Pair	Order Ticket #	Buy/ Sell	Lots/ Units	Entry Price	Exit Price	Close Date/Time	Pips W/L	Profit/ Loss	New Balance

TRADE SETUP NOTES:

ADDITIONAL NOTES:

Order Date/Time	Pair	Order Ticket #	Buy/ Sell	Lots/ Units	Entry Price	Exit Price	Close Date/Time	Pips W/L	Profit/ Loss	New Balance

TRADE SETUP NOTES:

ADDITIONAL NOTES:

Order Date/Time	Pair	Order Ticket #	Buy/ Sell	Lots/ Units	Entry Price	Exit Price	Close Date/Time	Pips W/L	Profit/ Loss	New Balance

TRADE SETUP NOTES:

ADDITIONAL NOTES:

Order Date/Time	Pair	Order Ticket #	Buy/ Sell	Lots/ Units	Entry Price	Exit Price	Close Date/Time	Pips W/L	Profit/ Loss	New Balance

TRADE SETUP NOTES:

ADDITIONAL NOTES:

Order Date/Time	Pair	Order Ticket #	Buy/ Sell	Lots/ Units	Entry Price	Exit Price	Close Date/Time	Pips W/L	Profit/ Loss	New Balance

TRADE SETUP NOTES:

ADDITIONAL NOTES:

Order Date/Time	Pair	Order Ticket #	Buy/ Sell	Lots/ Units	Entry Price	Exit Price	Close Date/Time	Pips W/L	Profit/ Loss	New Balance

TRADE SETUP NOTES:

ADDITIONAL NOTES:

Order Date/Time	Pair	Order Ticket #	Buy/ Sell	Lots/ Units	Entry Price	Exit Price	Close Date/Time	Pips W/L	Profit/ Loss	New Balance

TRADE SETUP NOTES:

ADDITIONAL NOTES:

TRADING LOG

Order Date/Time	Pair	Order Ticket #	Buy/ Sell	Lots/ Units	Entry Price	Exit Price	Close Date/Time	Pips W/L	Profit/ Loss	New Balance

TRADE SETUP NOTES:

ADDITIONAL NOTES:

Order Date/Time	Pair	Order Ticket #	Buy/ Sell	Lots/ Units	Entry Price	Exit Price	Close Date/Time	Pips W/L	Profit/ Loss	New Balance

TRADE SETUP NOTES:

ADDITIONAL NOTES:

Order Date/Time	Pair	Order Ticket #	Buy/ Sell	Lots/ Units	Entry Price	Exit Price	Close Date/Time	Pips W/L	Profit/ Loss	New Balance

TRADE SETUP NOTES:

ADDITIONAL NOTES:

Order Date/Time	Pair	Order Ticket #	Buy/ Sell	Lots/ Units	Entry Price	Exit Price	Close Date/Time	Pips W/L	Profit/ Loss	New Balance

TRADE SETUP NOTES:

ADDITIONAL NOTES:

Order Date/Time	Pair	Order Ticket #	Buy/ Sell	Lots/ Units	Entry Price	Exit Price	Close Date/Time	Pips W/L	Profit/ Loss	New Balance

TRADE SETUP NOTES:

ADDITIONAL NOTES:

Order Date/Time	Pair	Order Ticket #	Buy/ Sell	Lots/ Units	Entry Price	Exit Price	Close Date/Time	Pips W/L	Profit/ Loss	New Balance

TRADE SETUP NOTES:

ADDITIONAL NOTES:

TRADING LOG

Order Date/Time	Pair	Order Ticket #	Buy/ Sell	Lots/ Units	Entry Price	Exit Price	Close Date/Time	Pips W/L	Profit/ Loss	New Balance

TRADE SETUP NOTES:

ADDITIONAL NOTES:

Order Date/Time	Pair	Order Ticket #	Buy/ Sell	Lots/ Units	Entry Price	Exit Price	Close Date/Time	Pips W/L	Profit/ Loss	New Balance

TRADE SETUP NOTES:

ADDITIONAL NOTES:

Order Date/Time	Pair	Order Ticket #	Buy/ Sell	Lots/ Units	Entry Price	Exit Price	Close Date/Time	Pips W/L	Profit/ Loss	New Balance

TRADE SETUP NOTES:

ADDITIONAL NOTES:

Order Date/Time	Pair	Order Ticket #	Buy/ Sell	Lots/ Units	Entry Price	Exit Price	Close Date/Time	Pips W/L	Profit/ Loss	New Balance

TRADE SETUP NOTES:

ADDITIONAL NOTES:

Order Date/Time	Pair	Order Ticket #	Buy/ Sell	Lots/ Units	Entry Price	Exit Price	Close Date/Time	Pips W/L	Profit/ Loss	New Balance

TRADE SETUP NOTES:

ADDITIONAL NOTES:

Order Date/Time	Pair	Order Ticket #	Buy/ Sell	Lots/ Units	Entry Price	Exit Price	Close Date/Time	Pips W/L	Profit/ Loss	New Balance

TRADE SETUP NOTES:

ADDITIONAL NOTES:

Order Date/Time	Pair	Order Ticket #	Buy/ Sell	Lots/ Units	Entry Price	Exit Price	Close Date/Time	Pips W/L	Profit/ Loss	New Balance

TRADE SETUP NOTES:

ADDITIONAL NOTES:

TRADING LOG

Order Date/Time	Pair	Order Ticket #	Buy/ Sell	Lots/ Units	Entry Price	Exit Price	Close Date/Time	Pips W/L	Profit/ Loss	New Balance

TRADE SETUP NOTES:

ADDITIONAL NOTES:

Order Date/Time	Pair	Order Ticket #	Buy/ Sell	Lots/ Units	Entry Price	Exit Price	Close Date/Time	Pips W/L	Profit/ Loss	New Balance

TRADE SETUP NOTES:

ADDITIONAL NOTES:

Order Date/Time	Pair	Order Ticket #	Buy/ Sell	Lots/ Units	Entry Price	Exit Price	Close Date/Time	Pips W/L	Profit/ Loss	New Balance

TRADE SETUP NOTES:

ADDITIONAL NOTES:

Order Date/Time	Pair	Order Ticket #	Buy/ Sell	Lots/ Units	Entry Price	Exit Price	Close Date/Time	Pips W/L	Profit/ Loss	New Balance

TRADE SETUP NOTES:

ADDITIONAL NOTES:

Order Date/Time	Pair	Order Ticket #	Buy/ Sell	Lots/ Units	Entry Price	Exit Price	Close Date/Time	Pips W/L	Profit/ Loss	New Balance

TRADE SETUP NOTES:

ADDITIONAL NOTES:

Order Date/Time	Pair	Order Ticket #	Buy/ Sell	Lots/ Units	Entry Price	Exit Price	Close Date/Time	Pips W/L	Profit/ Loss	New Balance

TRADE SETUP NOTES:

ADDITIONAL NOTES:

TRADING LOG

Order Date/Time	Pair	Order Ticket #	Buy/ Sell	Lots/ Units	Entry Price	Exit Price	Close Date/Time	Pips W/L	Profit/ Loss	New Balance

TRADE SETUP NOTES:

ADDITIONAL NOTES:

Order Date/Time	Pair	Order Ticket #	Buy/ Sell	Lots/ Units	Entry Price	Exit Price	Close Date/Time	Pips W/L	Profit/ Loss	New Balance

TRADE SETUP NOTES:

ADDITIONAL NOTES:

Order Date/Time	Pair	Order Ticket #	Buy/ Sell	Lots/ Units	Entry Price	Exit Price	Close Date/Time	Pips W/L	Profit/ Loss	New Balance

TRADE SETUP NOTES:

ADDITIONAL NOTES:

Order Date/Time	Pair	Order Ticket #	Buy/ Sell	Lots/ Units	Entry Price	Exit Price	Close Date/Time	Pips W/L	Profit/ Loss	New Balance

TRADE SETUP NOTES:

ADDITIONAL NOTES:

Order Date/Time	Pair	Order Ticket #	Buy/ Sell	Lots/ Units	Entry Price	Exit Price	Close Date/Time	Pips W/L	Profit/ Loss	New Balance

TRADE SETUP NOTES:

ADDITIONAL NOTES:

Order Date/Time	Pair	Order Ticket #	Buy/ Sell	Lots/ Units	Entry Price	Exit Price	Close Date/Time	Pips W/L	Profit/ Loss	New Balance

TRADE SETUP NOTES:

ADDITIONAL NOTES:

TRADING LOG

Order Date/Time	Pair	Order Ticket #	Buy/ Sell	Lots/ Units	Entry Price	Exit Price	Close Date/Time	Pips W/L	Profit/ Loss	New Balance

TRADE SETUP NOTES:

ADDITIONAL NOTES:

Order Date/Time	Pair	Order Ticket #	Buy/ Sell	Lots/ Units	Entry Price	Exit Price	Close Date/Time	Pips W/L	Profit/ Loss	New Balance

TRADE SETUP NOTES:

ADDITIONAL NOTES:

Order Date/Time	Pair	Order Ticket #	Buy/ Sell	Lots/ Units	Entry Price	Exit Price	Close Date/Time	Pips W/L	Profit/ Loss	New Balance

TRADE SETUP NOTES:

ADDITIONAL NOTES:

Order Date/Time	Pair	Order Ticket #	Buy/ Sell	Lots/ Units	Entry Price	Exit Price	Close Date/Time	Pips W/L	Profit/ Loss	New Balance

TRADE SETUP NOTES:

ADDITIONAL NOTES:

Order Date/Time	Pair	Order Ticket #	Buy/ Sell	Lots/ Units	Entry Price	Exit Price	Close Date/Time	Pips W/L	Profit/ Loss	New Balance

TRADE SETUP NOTES:

ADDITIONAL NOTES:

Order Date/Time	Pair	Order Ticket #	Buy/ Sell	Lots/ Units	Entry Price	Exit Price	Close Date/Time	Pips W/L	Profit/ Loss	New Balance

TRADE SETUP NOTES:

ADDITIONAL NOTES:

TRADING LOG

Order Date/Time	Pair	Order Ticket #	Buy/ Sell	Lots/ Units	Entry Price	Exit Price	Close Date/Time	Pips W/L	Profit/ Loss	New Balance

TRADE SETUP NOTES:

ADDITIONAL NOTES:

Order Date/Time	Pair	Order Ticket #	Buy/ Sell	Lots/ Units	Entry Price	Exit Price	Close Date/Time	Pips W/L	Profit/ Loss	New Balance

TRADE SETUP NOTES:

ADDITIONAL NOTES:

Order Date/Time	Pair	Order Ticket #	Buy/ Sell	Lots/ Units	Entry Price	Exit Price	Close Date/Time	Pips W/L	Profit/ Loss	New Balance

TRADE SETUP NOTES:

ADDITIONAL NOTES:

Order Date/Time	Pair	Order Ticket #	Buy/ Sell	Lots/ Units	Entry Price	Exit Price	Close Date/Time	Pips W/L	Profit/ Loss	New Balance

TRADE SETUP NOTES:

ADDITIONAL NOTES:

Order Date/Time	Pair	Order Ticket #	Buy/ Sell	Lots/ Units	Entry Price	Exit Price	Close Date/Time	Pips W/L	Profit/ Loss	New Balance

TRADE SETUP NOTES:

ADDITIONAL NOTES:

Order Date/Time	Pair	Order Ticket #	Buy/ Sell	Lots/ Units	Entry Price	Exit Price	Close Date/Time	Pips W/L	Profit/ Loss	New Balance

TRADE SETUP NOTES:

ADDITIONAL NOTES:

TRADING LOG

Order Date/Time	Pair	Order Ticket #	Buy/Sell	Lots/Units	Entry Price	Exit Price	Close Date/Time	Pips W/L	Profit/Loss	New Balance

TRADE SETUP NOTES:

ADDITIONAL NOTES:

Order Date/Time	Pair	Order Ticket #	Buy/Sell	Lots/Units	Entry Price	Exit Price	Close Date/Time	Pips W/L	Profit/Loss	New Balance

TRADE SETUP NOTES:

ADDITIONAL NOTES:

Order Date/Time	Pair	Order Ticket #	Buy/Sell	Lots/Units	Entry Price	Exit Price	Close Date/Time	Pips W/L	Profit/Loss	New Balance

TRADE SETUP NOTES:

ADDITIONAL NOTES:

Order Date/Time	Pair	Order Ticket #	Buy/Sell	Lots/Units	Entry Price	Exit Price	Close Date/Time	Pips W/L	Profit/Loss	New Balance

TRADE SETUP NOTES:

ADDITIONAL NOTES:

Order Date/Time	Pair	Order Ticket #	Buy/Sell	Lots/Units	Entry Price	Exit Price	Close Date/Time	Pips W/L	Profit/Loss	New Balance

TRADE SETUP NOTES:

ADDITIONAL NOTES:

Order Date/Time	Pair	Order Ticket #	Buy/Sell	Lots/Units	Entry Price	Exit Price	Close Date/Time	Pips W/L	Profit/Loss	New Balance

TRADE SETUP NOTES:

ADDITIONAL NOTES:

TRADING LOG

Order Date/Time	Pair	Order Ticket #	Buy/ Sell	Lots/ Units	Entry Price	Exit Price	Close Date/Time	Pips W/L	Profit/ Loss	New Balance

TRADE SETUP NOTES:

ADDITIONAL NOTES:

Order Date/Time	Pair	Order Ticket #	Buy/ Sell	Lots/ Units	Entry Price	Exit Price	Close Date/Time	Pips W/L	Profit/ Loss	New Balance

TRADE SETUP NOTES:

ADDITIONAL NOTES:

Order Date/Time	Pair	Order Ticket #	Buy/ Sell	Lots/ Units	Entry Price	Exit Price	Close Date/Time	Pips W/L	Profit/ Loss	New Balance

TRADE SETUP NOTES:

ADDITIONAL NOTES:

Order Date/Time	Pair	Order Ticket #	Buy/ Sell	Lots/ Units	Entry Price	Exit Price	Close Date/Time	Pips W/L	Profit/ Loss	New Balance

TRADE SETUP NOTES:

ADDITIONAL NOTES:

Order Date/Time	Pair	Order Ticket #	Buy/ Sell	Lots/ Units	Entry Price	Exit Price	Close Date/Time	Pips W/L	Profit/ Loss	New Balance

TRADE SETUP NOTES:

ADDITIONAL NOTES:

Order Date/Time	Pair	Order Ticket #	Buy/ Sell	Lots/ Units	Entry Price	Exit Price	Close Date/Time	Pips W/L	Profit/ Loss	New Balance

TRADE SETUP NOTES:

ADDITIONAL NOTES:

Order Date/Time	Pair	Order Ticket #	Buy/ Sell	Lots/ Units	Entry Price	Exit Price	Close Date/Time	Pips W/L	Profit/ Loss	New Balance

TRADE SETUP NOTES:

ADDITIONAL NOTES:

TRADING LOG

Order Date/Time	Pair	Order Ticket #	Buy/ Sell	Lots/ Units	Entry Price	Exit Price	Close Date/Time	Pips W/L	Profit/ Loss	New Balance

TRADE SETUP NOTES:

ADDITIONAL NOTES:

Order Date/Time	Pair	Order Ticket #	Buy/ Sell	Lots/ Units	Entry Price	Exit Price	Close Date/Time	Pips W/L	Profit/ Loss	New Balance

TRADE SETUP NOTES:

ADDITIONAL NOTES:

Order Date/Time	Pair	Order Ticket #	Buy/ Sell	Lots/ Units	Entry Price	Exit Price	Close Date/Time	Pips W/L	Profit/ Loss	New Balance

TRADE SETUP NOTES:

ADDITIONAL NOTES:

Order Date/Time	Pair	Order Ticket #	Buy/ Sell	Lots/ Units	Entry Price	Exit Price	Close Date/Time	Pips W/L	Profit/ Loss	New Balance

TRADE SETUP NOTES:

ADDITIONAL NOTES:

Order Date/Time	Pair	Order Ticket #	Buy/ Sell	Lots/ Units	Entry Price	Exit Price	Close Date/Time	Pips W/L	Profit/ Loss	New Balance

TRADE SETUP NOTES:

ADDITIONAL NOTES:

Order Date/Time	Pair	Order Ticket #	Buy/ Sell	Lots/ Units	Entry Price	Exit Price	Close Date/Time	Pips W/L	Profit/ Loss	New Balance

TRADE SETUP NOTES:

ADDITIONAL NOTES:

TRADING LOG

Order Date/Time	Pair	Order Ticket #	Buy/ Sell	Lots/ Units	Entry Price	Exit Price	Close Date/Time	Pips W/L	Profit/ Loss	New Balance

TRADE SETUP NOTES:

ADDITIONAL NOTES:

Order Date/Time	Pair	Order Ticket #	Buy/ Sell	Lots/ Units	Entry Price	Exit Price	Close Date/Time	Pips W/L	Profit/ Loss	New Balance

TRADE SETUP NOTES:

ADDITIONAL NOTES:

Order Date/Time	Pair	Order Ticket #	Buy/ Sell	Lots/ Units	Entry Price	Exit Price	Close Date/Time	Pips W/L	Profit/ Loss	New Balance

TRADE SETUP NOTES:

ADDITIONAL NOTES:

Order Date/Time	Pair	Order Ticket #	Buy/ Sell	Lots/ Units	Entry Price	Exit Price	Close Date/Time	Pips W/L	Profit/ Loss	New Balance

TRADE SETUP NOTES:

ADDITIONAL NOTES:

Order Date/Time	Pair	Order Ticket #	Buy/ Sell	Lots/ Units	Entry Price	Exit Price	Close Date/Time	Pips W/L	Profit/ Loss	New Balance

TRADE SETUP NOTES:

ADDITIONAL NOTES:

Order Date/Time	Pair	Order Ticket #	Buy/ Sell	Lots/ Units	Entry Price	Exit Price	Close Date/Time	Pips W/L	Profit/ Loss	New Balance

TRADE SETUP NOTES:

ADDITIONAL NOTES:

Order Date/Time	Pair	Order Ticket #	Buy/ Sell	Lots/ Units	Entry Price	Exit Price	Close Date/Time	Pips W/L	Profit/ Loss	New Balance

TRADE SETUP NOTES:

ADDITIONAL NOTES:

TRADING LOG

Order Date/Time	Pair	Order Ticket #	Buy/ Sell	Lots/ Units	Entry Price	Exit Price	Close Date/Time	Pips W/L	Profit/ Loss	New Balance

TRADE SETUP NOTES:

ADDITIONAL NOTES:

Order Date/Time	Pair	Order Ticket #	Buy/ Sell	Lots/ Units	Entry Price	Exit Price	Close Date/Time	Pips W/L	Profit/ Loss	New Balance

TRADE SETUP NOTES:

ADDITIONAL NOTES:

Order Date/Time	Pair	Order Ticket #	Buy/ Sell	Lots/ Units	Entry Price	Exit Price	Close Date/Time	Pips W/L	Profit/ Loss	New Balance

TRADE SETUP NOTES:

ADDITIONAL NOTES:

Order Date/Time	Pair	Order Ticket #	Buy/ Sell	Lots/ Units	Entry Price	Exit Price	Close Date/Time	Pips W/L	Profit/ Loss	New Balance

TRADE SETUP NOTES:

ADDITIONAL NOTES:

Order Date/Time	Pair	Order Ticket #	Buy/ Sell	Lots/ Units	Entry Price	Exit Price	Close Date/Time	Pips W/L	Profit/ Loss	New Balance

TRADE SETUP NOTES:

ADDITIONAL NOTES:

Order Date/Time	Pair	Order Ticket #	Buy/ Sell	Lots/ Units	Entry Price	Exit Price	Close Date/Time	Pips W/L	Profit/ Loss	New Balance

TRADE SETUP NOTES:

ADDITIONAL NOTES:

Order Date/Time	Pair	Order Ticket #	Buy/ Sell	Lots/ Units	Entry Price	Exit Price	Close Date/Time	Pips W/L	Profit/ Loss	New Balance

TRADE SETUP NOTES:

ADDITIONAL NOTES:

Made in the USA
Middletown, DE
28 June 2020